ASSIGNMENT: SPORTS

ASSIGNMENT: SPORTS

By ROBERT LIPSYTE

HARPER & ROW, PUBLISHERS
New York, Evanston, and London

ASSIGNMENT: SPORTS

Library of Congress Catalog Card Number: 77-85032

To the memory of James J. Kernan, teacher—
the man who said *Go*.

Contents

ASSIGNMENT:
SPORTS

SPRING

Down on the field, Met fans were screaming "We're Number One" and tearing out hunks of earth and grass to take home, and across the East River in Manhattan, paper was raining out of skyscraper windows. The Shea Stadium scoreboard clock read a few minutes after three on this Thursday, October 16, 1969, but my mind was more than seven years and a thousand miles away.

The Mets' first spring training, in 1962, was my first major assignment as a sports reporter for *The New York Times*. I had been on the *Times* for nearly five years, restless for a big story. After graduation from Columbia College in June, 1957, I answered an advertisement for a copyboy in the *Times'* sports department. In September, 1959, I was promoted to reporter, but I spent almost all of my time in the office, at night, rewriting press releases and taking other men's stories over the telephone. I rarely got more than a mile from the office on assignment, and then only in an emergency.

Then the sports editor, James Roach, asked me one day if I would like to go to Florida and cover this new baseball team.

Would I?

Now I was in the press box, a columnist, when the Mets won the World Series. I had been to a lot of places during those seven and a half years. But I remember none so well as that first big assignment, the real beginning for me, which came, fittingly enough, in the spring, the start of the sportswriter's year.

I

John Pappas Tries Out
for the Mets

John Pappas appeared on the second day of spring training. He was thin and pale, and he looked about seventeen years old. He said he was twenty-one and that he had come to St. Petersburg, Florida, to be a pitcher for the New York Mets. Nobody knew what to do with him.

In any other major league clubhouse that spring, the equipment manager or the assistant trainer or maybe even the bat boy would have heaved John Pappas out the door. But this was the second day of the Mets' very first spring, and no one was sure enough of his own job to make a decision about someone else. So Pappas just stood quietly in the hushed, green-carpeted clubhouse, his sneakers under one arm, his glove under the other.

Out on the field, a collection of strangers with hopes was trying to sort itself into a team. Rabbit-quick rookies made impossible leaping catches—always when the coaches weren't looking—and the older players, some of whom had once been stars with other teams, tried to sweat themselves down into shape for the long season ahead. The borderline players worked hardest of all, running extra laps around the outfield, taking long turns in the batting cage, and chattering "Attaboy, baby, show him the hummer, good hands, chuck it in there," because Casey Stengel, manager of the Mets, had a reputation for favoring players with spirit and hustle. The borderline players knew if they didn't make it with this brandnew team they would probably slide right on out of the major leagues.

Pappas stood for a long time in the clubhouse, politely but firmly telling anyone who asked that he had no intention of budging until someone from the Mets gave him a tryout. Finally, a tall sad-faced man came out of a side office and looked into Pappas' steady brown eyes. He introduced himself as John Murphy, an official of the new club.

"Where are you from?" asked Murphy.

"New York City," said Pappas.

"When was the last time you threw a ball?"

"Last Sunday, in New York," said Pappas.

Murphy's eyes narrowed, and he smiled, a triumphant little smile. "It snowed in New York last Sunday."

Pappas nodded. "Yes, sir. But not underneath the Triborough Bridge."

Murphy's eyes widened. He motioned Pappas to a wooden bench in front of the lockers and sat down beside him. The young man said he had bought four regulation National League baseballs and pitched them at a painted square on a concrete wall under the bridge. After he was satisfied, he ran for several miles in a nearby park. Then he packed for spring training.

He had arrived in St. Petersburg at three o'clock that morning, he said, after his first airplane trip. It was also the first time he had ever been more than a hundred miles from his parents' home in Astoria, Queens.

Murphy listened and nodded and pulled at his long, sad face. Then he stood up. "We're not holding tryouts here, John." He pointed through the open clubhouse door to the practice ball fields. "There would be a million guys out there if we were."

"I don't see a million guys out there," said Pappas seriously and softly. When Murphy shot him a hard glance to see if he was being smart, Pappas looked down at his black pointy shoes.

Murphy sighed. "You play high-school ball?"

"My high school didn't have a team, Mr. Murphy, but I played Police Athletic League ball. I don't remember which precinct."

"Did anyone ever say you were professional material?"

"No, sir."

"Do your parents know you came down here for a tryout?"

"No one knows, Mr. Murphy."

Murphy sat down again, and his voice became gentle. "Do you go to school?"

"I was going to City College at night, but I stopped going to classes. And I quit my job. I was working in a furniture store. I told my mother I was coming down for a week's vacation and then I'd look for another job."

Almost wearily, Murphy said, "This is not a tryout camp."

Pappas took a deep breath. "Mr. Murphy, I don't have much experience, and I'm willing to spend a few years in the minors. But I think I can pitch, and I want to find out now. I want to succeed in the world, and I can do it if I set my mind to it."

"Of course you can," said Murphy, "but there are many ways to succeed in the world besides major league baseball."

"I'm going to stay here until someone looks at me pitch," said Pappas, running a bony hand through his black pompadour. "If they tell me I'm no good, I'll just finish my vacation and go home and set my mind to something else."

Murphy stared at Pappas for a long time. "Okay, John," he said. "You get yourself a catcher and a place to throw and call me up and I'll come over and look at you."

They shook hands, and Pappas, smiling now, bounded out of the clubhouse. "Thanks, thanks a lot," he called back over his shoulder. "I'll see you soon."

Murphy watched him go, then shook his head at us and walked back into his office. Another newspaperman turned to me and said, "That's a flaky kid for you. I don't know why Murphy wastes his time."

"What do you mean flaky?" I said. "He might really have it; he might be a star. And who says Murphy could tell from one tryout?"

"Johnny Murphy was once a great relief pitcher for the Yankees," said the other newspaperman, "and I think you're a flaky kid, too."

The weather was erratic in St. Petersburg that week, sometimes cool, almost always windy. John Pappas ran in the mornings near his motel and found youngsters to catch his pitching. Three days after he first showed up, a local newspaper arranged for Pappas to use a nearby high-school ball field, and Murphy promised to drive out to watch him pitch. Murphy said he would even bring a professional catcher.

The morning of his tryout Pappas returned to the Mets spring-training camp at Miller Huggins Field and found a seat in the sun on the grandstand. A little less pale now, but still thin and tense, he sat in a crowd of elderly tourists and pensioners and watched the Mets work out. I sat with him for a little while. He pointed at four young Met pitchers who were taking turns throwing for batting practice.

"That could be me," he said.

At 3:38 P.M. on February 23, 1962, John Pappas had his chance. While a dozen newspapermen and photographers watched, he strode onto a scruffy pitching mound and put everything in his slight body behind the baseballs he threw at Bill Whalen, a young catcher from the Mets' camp. Pappas threw for eighteen minutes in silence. He was wild, and he wasn't very fast.

At precisely 3:56 P.M., Murphy walked out to the mound and put his arm around Pappas' thin shoulders. "All you have is guts, son," he said.

They shook hands. Murphy thanked Pappas for giving the Mets a chance to look him over. Very kindly, he told Pappas to forget about professional baseball. Maybe if he were only fifteen years old it might make sense to keep at it, but at twenty-one he had too far to go and too much to learn.

Pappas thanked Murphy for giving him a tryout. He said he was satisfied and now he was going back to New York.

"I always would have wondered," said Pappas, "but now I know. I just wasn't good enough. Now I'll look for something else, some other way of being somebody."

The ball field slowly emptied, and soon there was just Pappas, and two or three of the younger newspapermen who had secretly hoped that this thin, sallow, round-shouldered young clerk would turn out to have an arm like a bullwhip, a live fastball that hummed, and a curve that danced in the sun. I think we were more disappointed than he was, and we were talking mostly for ourselves on the ride back to town, telling Pappas that there were other ways to succeed in the world besides major league baseball and that he was way ahead of the game; after all, how many men actually get a chance to try out, to find out once and for all? Pappas nodded and agreed and smiled and thanked us for our encouragement.

It was dusk when we reached his motel. The last time I saw John Pappas he was framed in the car window, and he said: "You know, I'm sorry they didn't give me a chance to hit. I'm not a bad hitter. And I play the outfield too."

II

A Yankee Manager Looks Them Over

For the sportswriter, the cycle of the year begins in late February in California or Arizona or Florida when the baseball teams open their spring training camps. Technically, it is still winter. But everyone's dream is fresh, all hopes are possibilities, and the best time of the year lies ahead. Truly, it is spring.

In 1967, five years after the Mets and John Pappas and I made our spring training debuts together, I went south again to cover a baseball camp. This time the team was the Yankees and the city was Fort Lauderdale. And I still had a lot to learn.

The young pitcher looked very sharp at breakfast. His lean jaw was freshly shaven, he was wearing a clean sport shirt, and there was an unaccountably jaunty bounce to his step. Baseball players are notoriously stingy tippers, and the Yankee management had suggested that players leave at least twenty-five cents for the breakfast waiter in the team dining room. The young pitcher left fifty cents.

Instead of waiting for the team bus out to the ball field, the young pitcher hitched an early ride with one of the coaches.

He was sitting in front of his wooden locker, pounding his glove and making bright small talk with the trainers and sporting-goods salesmen, when the rest of the Yankees straggled into the clubhouse, sleepy-eyed, lead-footed, in their usual morning grump.

After the routine ten-minute morning meeting with the manager and the coaches, the young pitcher was the first player out on the field. He did more sit-ups than anyone else during the brief exercise session on the outfield grass. He kept moving fast through the hot morning until his gray uniform was black with sweat.

When it was his turn to pitch batting practice, he poured in the hummer and the smoker and then ran windsprints as if he were training for the Olympics instead of the baseball season. When the pitchers were sent out to shag fly balls, he raced in for every blooper and made fantastic one-handed catches against the outfield walls. The other pitchers were clumped together for shoptalk and gossip, pretending not to see the fly balls.

When the pitchers were brought in for infield practice, he charged every ground ball and went diving for line drives. The other pitchers just waved at the grounders skipping by and looked at the young pitcher as if he were sunstruck.

"That man," I said to Yankee manager Ralph Houk, "is really hustling."

"That man," snapped Houk, "is really guilty. He wasn't thinking about baseball last night."

"How can you tell?"

"You know," said Houk, "it's really pitiful how easy

it is to see when a man's trying to con you. Just looking at a man, you know what kind of night he had. Maybe he's dragging his tail. Or maybe like your friend out there he's working just a little too hard, trying to cover up." Houk grinned. "I've been through it myself. When I think back, I can see how foolish I must have looked."

Coaches and managers can tell pretty quickly whether or not a pitcher has "the live hose," if an infielder has "the good hands," if an outfielder has "the big bat and the good wheels." Yet until the exhibition season begins, they can't really judge a player's reaction under pressure —if he's a "clutch" player or a man who "chokes." But there's ample time during the early days of spring training to find out whether a player is drenched in honest noonday sweat or last night's Scotch.

There was no bed check for the Yankees during the spring, no hard-and-fast curfew. The players were usually finished for the day by 2 P.M. They showered, changed back into their casual sport clothes, and spent a few hours before dinner relaxing on the golf course or the fishing pier or perhaps window-shopping downtown, or, more often, propped up in bed, watching television in their air-conditioned motel rooms.

Spring trainings have produced automobile accidents, bar brawls, and headlined romances. But that spring of 1967 was a strictly-business spring. The Yankees had finished in tenth place the previous season, and most of the stars of the world-championship years were gone. There was no complacency, and many youngsters were competing for each position.

There have been legendary players who could carouse all night and hit home runs all day, but today's players seem lesser men who have difficulty doing either well. Or so the nostalgic old-timers told me.

More important perhaps, there are now more college-educated ballplayers, all looking beyond their major-league years to second careers in insurance, investment counseling, social work, teaching, or public relations. They are serious young men who bring their wives and children to spring training if they can.

"It's all right out in the open," said Houk, the manager, chuckling softly at the end of the day's workout. "That's one thing about sports. A man succeeds, a man fails, a man hustles or dogs it, it's plain to see right in front of you."

He discreetly nodded toward the young pitcher dragging himself off the field, mouth open, shoulders sagging, legs buckling.

"I have a feeling," said Houk, "that young man is going to be asleep tonight long before I am."

III

A Legacy for Tom Tresh

One afternoon during that spring in Fort Lauderdale, the Yankee left-fielder, Tom Tresh, came into the dugout for a cup of water. It was cool in the dugout, and some of us were sitting there talking. Tom sat down, hooked his elbows on the back of the dugout bench, and stretched his long legs. After a while the conversation moved his way, and soon he was talking softly about his father, Mike Tresh, who had died a few months before of heart disease and cancer. Mike Tresh was fifty-two when he died, and Tom was twenty-eight. Mike had once been a major-league catcher and had always been very involved in Tom's career. Now for the first season Tom was in training alone.

"When I was very young," said Tom, "my father and I played ping-pong—very fierce, competitive games. He always won. I remember once I went crying to my mother. I complained to her that he always won and never gave me a break. My father overheard. He said to me, 'Someday you'll beat me, Tom, and when you do, you'll know you did it by yourself.'"

Tom's first year with the Yankees, 1962, was a big one. He was named American League Rookie of the Year, and he won a World Series game with a home run. The pride

13

in Mike Tresh's face shone from the front pages of newspapers across the country.

"He lived for me," said Tom, "and I feel so fortunate
that I could do well for him. I always felt sorry for Mickey
Mantle in that his father died before he could see Mickey
achieve his greatness. But my father was able to see my
success, and then two years ago I had a grandson for
him, Michael."

Tom shifted on the bench, unhooked his elbows, and
planted them on his knees. "I knew he was dying last
year. He was in great discomfort. It was so hard to watch
this powerful man fading away.

"Whenever the club went to Detroit, I stayed at my
parents' house, and my father came out to the ball park.
It's funny how things turn out. In the last game we
played in Detroit last year, I got up to bat, and I wanted
to hit a home run for my father. I knew it would probably
be the last time he'd ever see me play.

"At that moment I never wanted to do anything so
badly as hit that home run. And I hit one. When I came
across the plate, I looked for him in the stands. He wasn't
there. He had gotten cold and gone down to the clubhouse. He heard it on radio."

Tom stood up. "Some things never die. The most important years are the younger years, when you're being
trained. I'll always have what he instilled in me then. He
was a great competitor, my father. He hated to lose, and
he taught me to lose graciously but to hate it."

"Tom," I asked him before he ran back to the outfield,
"how did you feel when you finally beat him in ping-
pong? Were you sad?"

"No, it was a great day," said Tom. "It was the day he had trained me for. But, you know, my father and I went fishing a lot. He was a competitor about that too—who could catch the most fish, the biggest fish. And I tried very hard, but I never could beat him in fishing."

IV

Lobby-Sitting with a Tough Old Pro

One night in St. Petersburg during the Mets' first spring training season, Rogers Hornsby leaned toward me, his thin lips a scar across his square face, his eyes a hostile ice-chip blue. "You planning on writing an article about me?"

I said that I was.

"You better quote me right," he said. "I'll read it, and if I don't like it, I'll be on your back so fast you won't know what happened."

Satisfied that he had intimidated me, Rogers Hornsby relaxed in an overstuffed lobby chair. It was a normal weekday evening during spring training, and Hornsby was holding court in his normal weekday-evening hang-out—a hotel lobby. He was sixty-six years old then—tall, straight, husky, and vigorous—and his hobby, as listed in the Baseball Register, had remained the same for forty-five years—lobby-sitting.

"I'm easy to get along with if you're on the up-and-up," said Hornsby in his flat cold voice, "but I'm not a good mixer. I get bored at parties, and I bore other people. I don't like to get dressed up and go out. I enjoy the right kind of people, my kind of people, but I don't like to do the sociable things. I think it's undignified, a man of my age going around in short pants, for example, and I don't think I'm old enough to play golf. I'm used to other people chasing balls I've hit. Damned if I'm going to run after a little ball myself."

Sitting in the lobby, hard and cold, Rogers Hornsby still looked the man who hit baseballs other people chased. Once he had been the most feared batsman in baseball, and many of his records still stand—official records for batting championships in the National League and the top single-season average of .424, and unofficial records for tactlessness, arrogance, and discourtesy.

One night, for example, when he was a player with the Giants, he was having dinner with a teammate, Ed Farrell. Someone stopped at the table and asked Hornsby if the Giants had a chance to win the pennant that year.

"Not with Farrell playing shortstop," snapped Hornsby.

Hornsby was soon sold to the Boston Braves as a player-manager. Early in the season he was asked if the Braves had a chance to win the pennant that year. Hornsby gestured contemptuously at his players.

"These humpty-dumpties?"

So on he went, from team to team to team. In 1952 he lasted exactly half a season with the St. Louis Browns. When the owner, Bill Veeck, fired Hornsby, the players chipped in and bought a silver trophy for Veeck. On it was inscribed:

TO BILL VEECK FOR THE GREATEST PLAY SINCE
THE EMANCIPATION PROCLAMATION, JUNE 10, 1952,
FROM THE PLAYERS OF THE ST. LOUIS BROWNS

But Hornsby got in the last word. Of Veeck, he said: "When you work for a screwball, you got to expect screwball tactics."

Rogers Hornsby returned to the big leagues in 1962 as batting coach for the New York Mets in their first season. His reputation had preceded him, and some of the players were a little worried. Was he still the arrogant old Hornsby, impatient with any man whose talent was less than his had been, or had he mellowed with time?

On the first day of batting drills, an outfielder named Joe Christopher ran up excitedly and blurted: "It's a great pleasure to meet you, Mr. Hornsby. For years I've been carrying around a magazine article with your batting tips."

The players around the batting cage edged forward to eavesdrop. They tensed when Hornsby snapped, "Did the tips help you any?"

Christopher said, "I didn't have anyone to work out with before."

Hornsby allowed himself a faint smile. "You'll get all the help you want now. Just holler."

The players relaxed. Hornsby had mellowed.

"How come," I asked him in the lobby that night, "you seem to have so many enemies in baseball?"

"Wouldn't want them phonies for friends anyway."

"But so many people call you narrow, bigoted, suspicious, and old-fashioned."

"Maybe because I'm not two-faced," said Hornsby. "I'm sure no diplomat. I say what I mean. Always did. From the start."

He had started in another era, born in a cattle town, Hornsby's Bend, Texas, where his grandfather had battled Indians and rustlers. He was raised in North Fort Worth after his father died. Baseball was a way out of the small town, and young Rogers followed his brother Everett, a spitball pitcher, into the Texas League. Everett never went much further, but in 1915 the St. Louis Cardinals barnstormed through Texas and were impressed with Rogers, a thin nineteen-year-old second baseman. They bought him for five hundred dollars, and they called him up to the big leagues that September.

"Hornsby," said the Cardinals' manager, "you're too skinny. I'm gonna have to farm you out on account of your size."

In baseball language, "farmed out" means sent to the minor leagues for further experience, but young Rogers thought it meant he would have to go to a farm. So he spent that winter on his uncle's farm in Lockhart, Texas, sleeping twelve hours a day and consuming great portions of ice cream, steak, milk, cheese, and potatoes. When he reported back to the Cardinals in the spring of 1916, he weighed one hundred and sixty-five pounds, thirty-five more than the previous season. He hit .313 that year—the first step toward the Hall of Fame.

Rogers Hornsby was also famous for his life style. He never smoked because "cigarettes cut down your wind." He never drank because "highballs are bad enough, but beer goes right to the legs and slows you up." He never went to movies because "it might affect my batting eye." And he never stayed out late with girls.

"I gotta get my sleep," he would explain. "The people pay money to see me at my best, not tired and hung over. I go out with girls—I'm human—but I figure if I don't get the pitch I want between 7 P.M. and midnight, forget it. I'll always get another chance to go to bat."

He never smoked or drank or stayed out late, but he had three wives, he was named in another man's divorce action, he punched a few men in the mouth, and he spent a great deal of money betting on the horses. Rogers Hornsby was no saint. But there was no doubt that he was devoted to baseball.

"Baseball is my life, the only thing I know and can talk about, my only interest," he said that night in spring training, his ice-blue eyes flicking around the hotel lobby. "People ask me what I do in the winter when there's no baseball. I'll tell you what I do. I sit and stare out the window and wait for spring."

Rogers Hornsby died a few years later, and when I heard of his death, I remembered him in his lobby chair, as tough as the oak and leather, no free smiles or diplomacy. And I remembered him standing stiff and solid by the batting cage, cold eyes shaded by yellow-tinted sunglasses, watching ballplayers who would never be half the batter he was but would make their way through life with greater ease. I remember one of those young players, in a friendly mood, pleasantly saying to the old coach, "What would you do, Mr. Hornsby, if you got in a batting slump?"

Hornsby snapped, "When you have a lifetime average of three-fifty-eight you don't have any slumps."

V

A Columbia Rower Pulls His Weight

When the ice breaks on the rivers of the north, rangy college men go down to the sea in fragile wooden peapods, determined to pull their weight. The sport, of course, is rowing, and the eight oarsmen and one coxswain in each racing shell are called the crew. Probably no other team sport in the world demands as much blind dedication, physical energy, and animal courage—and offers as little material reward and public recognition.

Richard Arthur Hansen was twenty-one years old in the spring of 1962. He had been rowing for Columbia for four years. His devotion had cost him most of the accepted by-products of college life: the dormitory bull sessions, the midnight parties, the casual flirtations over coffee. He could not care less.

"Years from now when I look back at college," he told me one afternoon on campus, "I will remember most the crew—the guys that I rowed with—and the days on the water. And that's what I'll miss most too."

Dick Hansen was born in suburban New Jersey. He played no sports at Hasbrouck Heights High School, spending his spare time clerking in a grocery store. He won an academic scholarship to Columbia College, and when he arrived he was 6 feet 1 inch tall, and 200 pounds fat.

During Freshman Orientation Week that fall of 1958, an assistant crew coach buttonholed him as he wandered, bewildered, around the campus. "How would you like to come out for crew?" asked the coach, impressed with Hansen's height.

Hansen barely knew what the man was talking about, but he said, "Yeah, sure. Why not?"

He had time to regret his words. A week later he was sitting in a sixteen-man barge, pulling a 12-foot oar through the garbage-littered Harlem River. He was drenched in the wake of passing sight-seeing boats, peppered from shore with rocks thrown by small boys, and harassed by coaches who yelled "Pull harder" just about the time he was telling himself "Dick, you're crazy; you hurt all over; you don't have to put up with this."

But he did. In late fall, the crew moved indoors. Three times a week, Dick ran three miles and went through an hour of muscle-wrenching calisthenics and then two or three ten-minute sessions in a simulated shell in the underground tank, trying to remember how his sliding seat worked, how to bring the blade of the oar back parallel to the water, and trying to forget the torn skin on his palms.

In late February, when the ice broke on the Harlem, the Columbia crew went outdoors again for spring practice. There were only twenty-seven heavyweight freshman left of the forty-five who had started. Now it was six days a week on the water, two hours a day of looking at the sweating back in front of him and wondering if he could keep rowing when his hands turned blue.

In the late spring, Dick made the Number Two position in the first freshman boat. He held it for three weeks before the stroke from the second boat beat him out for the slot. Dick was standing on the shore, a substitute, when his teammates competed in the big International Rowing Association regatta that June.

Dick lost more than thirty pounds his freshman year, barely got to meet any Barnard College girls, gave up all between-meal snacks, and always got to sleep by midnight on Saturday night. For what?

"It was wonderful then, and it still is," he said, his deep-set blue eyes faraway. "When eight guys are pulling together in unison and you see the puddles go by and you can tell that everybody is giving everything he has and the shell just seems to lift out of the water . . . well, you know everything is right with the world."

Between his freshman and sophomore years, Dick spent the summer clerking at the grocery store and exercising. In his second year at Columbia, he made the varsity. He disliked the coach that year, and he did not feel he made as much progress as he might have. But he never missed the 4:10 P.M. bus from 116th Street and Amsterdam Avenue to Baker Field in upper Manhattan, nor the 7 P.M. bus back to the dorms.

In his junior year, a new crew coach came to Columbia, a tough, militaristic former rower named Carl Ullrich. The new coach never raised his voice in anger or kept any man on the squad who missed a workout. Dick Hansen was delighted, and he rowed even harder.

"Poor guys," he would say of the blasé English majors

lolling about on campus while he went off to practice, "poor guys got the wrong information. They'll never know what they're missing."

A chemistry major, Dick was pulling a B average. As a member of the college's Naval Reserve Officers' Training Corps, he became a battalion personnel officer. Most important, he said, he felt part of something fine and secure.

"I'm part of a bunch of guys who've found out they can drive themselves long after they're exhausted, guys who've stuck it out. I've learned about everybody pulling out all the way, because the guys get ticked off if you don't pull your weight. It just means somebody else has to pull a little harder."

Crew members are clannish. They meet in the evenings for tea and a verbal re-row of races and practice. They have their private jokes; their own greetings. Together they ignore the boys who quit the crew, and they tolerate the rest of the world.

After his graduation, Dick Hansen and the other seniors on the varsity would probably never row again. But he will probably tell his sons someday of the tradition and mystiques of the crew. He may tell them about the mythical oarsman who slumped over his sweep near the end of the race and gasped, "I can't row another stroke." The rower behind tossed him overboard.

His sons will laugh at the tale—but for the wrong reasons. Hansen and all those who have rowed know the story is absurd: No oarsman would ever quit unless he were dead.

VI

Muhammad Ali: "I ain't losing nothing but gaining the world"

MIAMI BEACH, February 18, 1964. He was stretched out on a rubbing table, his chin propped on his fists, smiling at himself in a locker-room mirror. "You are beautiful," he said.

The steam from open shower stalls fogged the mirror and curled the pages of our notebooks.

"But what if you lose, Cassius; what happens then?" asked a columnist from Los Angeles.

"So beautiful," he said as his image faded in the steam. "Your publicity has overshadowed your talent. You are the double-greatest."

"Let's be serious for a minute," insisted a sportswriter from Boston. "What if the champ beats you?"

Cassius laughed into his fists. "I won't feel bad. I'll have tricked all the people into coming to the fight, to paying two hundred and fifty dollars for a ticket when they wouldn't have paid one hundred dollars without my talk."

"So this whole act," said the Boston man, "is just a con job, eh?"

"People ain't gonna give you nothing no way; you gotta go get it." He pushed up on the table, and his eyes sparkled. "I'm making all this money, the popcorn man making money, and the beer man, and you got something to write about; your papers let you come down to Miami Beach where it's warm."

The Boston man seemed a little angry at that. "Exactly what are you going to do when Sonny Liston beats you after all your big talk?"

"If Liston beats me, the next day I'll be on the sidewalk hollering 'No man ever beat me twice.' I'll be screaming for a rematch." The big brown body relaxed and seemed to melt into the rubbing table. The voice dropped to a whisper. "Or maybe I'll quit the ring for good. I'm twenty-two years old now." He closed his eyes. "I think I'm getting tired of fighting."

*   *   *

MIAMI BEACH, February 25, 1964. All evening, rumors swept the city that Cassius was not going to show up, that he had taken the step from hysteria to madness, that even now he was at the airport, waiting for a flight to Mexico City. Actually, while the rumors were at their height he was standing quietly in a far corner of Convention Hall, waiting for his brother, Rudy, to make his professional boxing debut.

Few people noticed him. He was wearing a tight-fitting black tropical suit, a black bow tie on his ruffled white dress shirt. He was surrounded by his trainers and aides and friends. Only once, in the second round when his brother knocked Chip Johnson down, did Cassius open his mouth. "That's it!" he yelled.

At the end of the fourth round, when it was announced

that Rudy had won his first professional fight, Cassius turned abruptly and followed a squad of Miami policemen with pearl-handled guns to his dressing room.

I went to my seat at ringside, where another reporter told me he did not believe Clay was en route to Mexico after all, he was still in his hotel room hiding under the bed.

* * *

NEW YORK, June 26, 1964. The long, black air-conditioned Cadillac limousine moved through Harlem, its dual speakers pounding out Marvin Gaye's version of "What's the Matter with You, Baby?" All the way down Lenox Avenue we stamped our feet and clapped our hands—the new champ, now known as Muhammad Ali; his brother, Rudy, now known as Rahman Ali; and their old friend from Louisville, Ronnie King, whose Muslim name was Omer Bey.

"Who is the champ?" sang out Muhammad.

"You is the champ," Rahman sang back.

"Who is that?"

"Muhammad Ali."

"Who's gonna be champ when Muhammad Ali retires?" sang out Muhammad Ali.

"I'm gonna be champ," Rahman sang back.

"But you ain't gonna fight Muhammad."

"No, sir!"

"You say he's too fast," sang out Muhammad.

"Too fast," Rahman sang back.

"You say he's the greatest."

"The greatest."

"You say you can't handle him."

"No, I can't handle him."

The limousine stopped at a red light, and Muhammad asked the chauffeur to play the Marvin Gaye record again. We rolled down all the windows, and when three pretty girls walked by, we started stamping our feet and clapping our hands again and singing along, "What's the matter with you, baby?"

*   *   *

STOCKHOLM, August 6, 1965. "Man, you just can't go strong all the time," he mumbled into his pillow, "can't be such a controversial figure, dodging all these traps . . ."

The hotel room was in Sweden, but it could have been anywhere: his clothes and boxing equipment strewn around the room, the portable stereo record player and a stack of 45's on the bureau. He had just fought an exhibition match at an amusement park in the city, and now, at midnight, he was tired from the boxing, the traveling, from the mounting pressures of his life.

"Just be myself." He was mumbling into the pillow, barely audible above the music of the record player. "Go out among the little people, the children and the folks sitting in garbage alleys, and they say 'That really you, Champ? You know you couldn't pay Chubby Checker and Joe Louis to come here and talk to us like you do.'

"That's what makes you powerful, the little people."

He kicked off his shoes and dug his toes into the mattress. "I live right and catch all this hell, don't drink or smoke or chase bad women. I treat everybody nice. You know, nobody ever came to me and said 'I'm going to become a Muslim because you are.' You have to live it and practice it and sacrifice and study. You don't love the cereal because Willie Mays eats it, but you might try it because of the man. But then you got to do the thing . . ." His voice began to trail off. "Life is a dream, boo-boo, boodey-boo . . ." and he was asleep.

* * *

LAS VEGAS, November 23, 1965. In the days leading up to the fight, Floyd Patterson had proclaimed himself an instant knight, a crusader fighting beneath the banners of Integration, Christianity, Goodness, and America who would wrest the heavyweight championship from the Black Muslim Ali. It was hard to feel sorry for Patterson when Ali, who had been careful not to reply in kind, took it out on the crusader's hide.

It was the cruelest fight I ever saw. For twelve rounds, until the referee stopped it, Ali mocked and humiliated and punished Patterson like a little boy pulling the wings off a butterfly, piecemeal. Throughout the fight Ali screamed "No contest, get me a contender" and "Boop, boop, boop" as his lightning jabs flicked out a little pain at a time. Whenever Patterson seemed about to collapse, Ali would let up the attack, giving the man time to recover enough to suffer some more.

The morning after the fight the two men sat side by side at a press conference, and Ali said to Patterson: "You should get honors and medals, the spot you was on, a good clean American boy fighting for America. All those movie stars behind you, they should make sure you never have to work another day in your life. It would be a disgrace on the government if you had to end up scuffling somewhere."

*   *   *

MIAMI, February 17, 1966. In the late afternoon when the air was sluggish and sweet, Muhammad Ali sat beneath a palm tree in front of his rented home and called to the passing children. He had finished working out for the day, and now, as the children came, the tension drained from his round face.

"Hey, little girl in the high-school sweater, you not gonna pass me by today."

"Hi, Cassius, how you been?"

"Fine. Whatcha learn in school today?"

The telephone rang inside the house. One of the three Muslim sisters who cooked for the champion and his entourage answered it. She called Ali to the phone. He went reluctantly.

When he returned, I saw that his face was twisted with rage.

"How can they do this to me?"

"What's that?"

"How can they reclassify me 1-A without another test to see if I'm wiser or worser than last time? Why are they so anxious? Why are they gunning for me?"

The sweetness drained out of the afternoon as red trucks from the television networks pulled up in front of the house, as the telephone rang continually, as reporters and photographers piled out of cars.

He jumped out of the lawn chair. "I've got a question," he said. "For two years the government caused me international embarrassment, letting people think I was a nut. Sure it bothered me, and my mother and father suffered, and now they jump up and make me 1-A without even a test. Why did they let me be considered a nut, an illiterate, for two years?"

No one had the answer for him. A television newscaster asked him what he thought about the war in Vietnam. Ali shrugged.

"Do you know where Vietnam is?"

"Sure," said Ali.

"Where?"

He shrugged.

"What do you think about the Vietcong?"

Ali shrugged again. "I got no quarrel with them Vietcong."

*   *   *

TORONTO, March 24, 1966. "The Americans are envious," said a young Dutchman, "because you speak the truth."

"Let other people defend me," said Ali, waving his arm, "because to defend myself would be cheapening."

Two Turkish visitors to his hotel room nodded, and Ali turned to them. "Am I well known in your country?"

"You are beloved," said one Turk. "On the streets of Istanbul, children wear pictures of you on their shirts, and cry 'I am the greatest.' "

"They do, really?"

"Yes," said the other Turk.

"Tell your people," said Ali, "that I will visit Turkey right after this fight with George Chuvalo."

"They will be very happy," said the second Turk. With that, bowing, he led the other two men out of the room.

Ali put his hands behind his head and hummed along with the record on the phonograph—Carla Thomas singing "Comfort Me." Then he said, "I am a jet."

"A what?" I asked.

"I am a jet, and all the rest is prop planes. Boxing will never be the same again. Once you been in a jet, you not ever really happy in a prop again."

*   *   *

LONDON, May 18, 1966. We were drinking tea in the Picadilly Hotel when three young black men with precise British diction, who said they were medical students, stopped by our table. They asked Ali to take his time beating up Henry Cooper in the championship match three days later. They asked Ali to please inflict suffering before knocking the white man out.

"And you're doctors?" asked Ali, setting down his teacup.

"We hope to be."

"Where you from?"

"He and I," said the spokesman, an intense chunky young man, "are from British Guiana. That one is from Ceylon."

"That right," said Ali, leaning back in his leather-covered chair. "Now, why you want me to hurt Cooper?"

"All this talk about Cooper's left hook and how he is

going to knock you out," said the chunky youth, shaking with anger.

"Oh, that," said Ali, grinning. "That's good."

"Good?" sputtered the medical students, so loudly that all the polite tea-drinkers looked up.

"Look here," said Ali. "You got to talk up a fight, say how vicious and dangerous this Cooper's left hook is, how the champion is scared—"

"But, Mr. Ali," said the Ceylonese, "he did knock you down last time."

"I was talking to the fans, not paying Cooper no attention," said Ali, brushing it aside. " 'The champion is scared,' the sportswriters write—they got to write something—'about this vicious left hook.' Now you got it?"

"You mean," asked the chunky student, "that Cooper does not possess a superior left hook?"

"It's all right," said Ali, shrugging. "The fans read what the sportswriters write about Cooper's vicious and dangerous left hook, and they start saying 'Man, we got to see this fight; this cat is going to knock the great Ali out.' They go and buy tickets, which cost money which go in my pocket. Now you got it?"

"In other words, Mr. Ali," said the Ceylonese carefully, "you approve of all this talk."

"You got it."

"Thank you, Mr. Ali," said the three students, moving away. They looked completely confused.

* * *

HOUSTON, February 5, 1967. The karate-trained

Fruit of Islam carefully searched everyone entering the
Muslim mosque, especially the half-dozen white reporters
and photographers. Our ball-point pens were taken apart;
nail files were confiscated. This is necessary, the Muslims
teach, because the truths of Elijah Muhammad are so
strong they can drive men crazy.

Raymond X, minister of the mosque, introduced the
main speaker as "another of Elijah's ministers and the
heavyweight champion of the world in that world." He
gestured toward "that world," a drab Negro neighbor-
hood beyond the auditorium window.

"Al-salàm, Alaykum!" said Muhammad Ali.

He told an audience of several hundred—most of
whom were non-Muslim Negroes curious to meet him—
that the teachings of Elijah had made him champion.
Heredity and talent had made him a good fighter, but the
Muslim teachings had kept him living clean and free
from temptation. He turned to the blackboard and con-
ducted a lesson on the evils of eating pork.

"The swine is the nastiest animal in the world," he
said, "a mouthful of maggots and pus. They bred the cat
and the rat and the dog and came up with the hog."

He then drew a sketch of a pig and imitated its snuf-
fling noises. He also told the audience that "dumb Negroes
come out dumber Negroes" after worshiping in Christian
churches. He said that Jesus Christ was dead, but the
Muslim God, Allah, was a living man.

"Other churches preach pie in the sky when you die,"
he said. "We want something sound while we're around
on the ground.

"I enjoy lecturing to you about the Honorable Elijah today more than I will whipping Ernie Terrell tomorrow."

After he had been speaking about fifteen minutes, the white newsmen were asked to leave.

*   *   *

NEW YORK, March 22, 1967. "Are you tense before a bout?" asked a man with a microphone a few minutes after the noon weigh-in for the fight with Zora Folley that night.

"Always tense, sometimes scared," snapped Ali, stomping off in his slush-stained work boots.

The broadcaster hurried after him. "Are you scared now?"

"Yup, scared," said Ali. "Anything can happen in a fight. Might trip going into the ring and break my arm."

*   *   *

CHICAGO, April 26, 1967. A spring storm lashed the city, and sheets of rain poured out of a bleak gray sky and roiled the waters of Lake Michigan. Through the plate-glass window of a motel coffee shop, Muhammad Ali watched the storm and moodily picked at three poached eggs on his plate.

"You think they'll give me poached eggs in jail?"

"I don't think so."

In two days he was scheduled to report to the Houston, Texas, draft-induction center. He would go, but he would refuse to take the one step forward that would turn him into Private Cassius Marcellus Clay, Jr. We wondered what would happen then. Would he be arrested on the spot and dragged off to jail, or would that just be the opening scene of months, maybe years, of legal maneuvers? And what would happen to his heavyweight title?

He had been up early that stormy April morning, arranging to store his gray Cadillac in a local garage and close out the motel room he kept as his Chicago home.

"I don't want to go to jail," he said, still staring out the rain-streaked window, "but I've got to live the life my conscience and my God tell me to. What does it profit me to be the wellest-liked man in America who sold out everybody?"

"Why don't you skip the country?"

"You serious? How long you been around me? I got to stay here and lead my people to the right man, Elijah Muhammad."

His tone was so absolute I felt slightly embarrassed. "Well, you've talked about someone so poisoned with hate he'd kill you and think he was doing the country a favor. It wouldn't serve any point, your getting killed."

Ali shook his head. "Every day they die in Vietnam for nothing. I might as well die right here for something."

Someone else at our table asked, "What about just playing the game like other big-time athletes? You wouldn't be sent to the front lines. You could give exhibitions and teach physical fitness."

Ali leaned across the table, his eyes suddenly bright, and he spoke very firmly. "What can you give me, America, for turning down my religion? You want me to do what the white man says and go fight a war against some people I don't know nothing about, get some freedom for some other people when my own can't get theirs here?"

Breakfast stretched into lunch as people came to our table, some to sit and talk, others merely to shake Ali's hand and wish him luck. Most were white men. Toward noon Ali's mood brightened, as the storm outside passed over the lake. The champion's eyes softened, and his voice deepened and dropped. He was going to play back a vision.

"Ah-lee will return," he intoned. "My ghost will haunt all arenas. The people will watch the fights, and they will whisper: *Hey, Ali could whip that guy . . . You think so? . . . Sure . . . No, he couldn't . . . Wish he'd come out of retirement.*"

His voice sharpened. "Twenty-five years old now. Make my comeback at twenty-eight. That's not old. Whip 'em all—if I get good food in jail. Don't you think?"

A newcomer to the table said it was all so very sad that such a handsome and gifted young man should have to contemplate death and imprisonment. Ali straightened, his eyes bright again, eyes of a martyr, reflecting the licking flames.

"Allah," he said, "okays the Adversary to try us. That's how he sees if you're a true believer."

He smiled. "All a man has to show for his time here on earth is what kind of name he had. Jesus. Columbus. Daniel Boone. Now, Wyatt Earp . . . who would have told him when he was fighting crooks and standing up for his principles that there'd be a television show about him? That the kids on the street would say 'I'm Wyatt Earp. *Reach.*' "

He half closed his eyes. His head lolled back. "Two thousand years from now," he whispered. And then he softly began to sing:

Muhammad Ali, Muhammad Ali,
He roamed the Western Hemisphere,
He was courageous and strong,
He called the round when the clown hit the ground.
Tell little children whatever they believe,
Stand up like Muhammad Ali.

*   *   *

SAN FRANCISCO, April 27, 1968. The sweet stench of marijuana floated out of the crowd in Civic Center Plaza and through the open windows of a blue Oldsmobile 98. The man behind the wheel, Jerry X, turned to the men in the back seat and said, "You could get stoned just breathing the air around this place."

Ali rolled his head, pretending to be stoned, and giggled in a strained falsetto. "Ladies, and, uh, gentlemen . . . we got a race problem in . . . uh, you got to excuse me, I'm as high as a kite."

Captain Jerry laughed and snapped another picture of Ali. Minister Majied smiled indulgently, but C. B. Atkins, a New York booking agent, stared out at the peace rally in the plaza, now swelling to about twelve thousand young people, and said, "I'll get you on right away so you don't have to wait."

"No," said Ali, "I'll wait for my time."

Captain Jerry laughed sharply. "Muhammad Ali, you'll wait for your time? The man is going to see you get time—time in jail."

A rock band finished its set on the wooden platform, and a man began shouting about peace in Vietnam. Ali shook his head. "I'm out on government bond; you not going to catch me talking about no war or draft-card burning or stuff like that. No, sir, I'm—Hey, look at those cats out there. There's one looks like he wants to raise some—Hey, there's one with plaits in his hair. My, oh, my. And look, I think I see one of the Smith Brothers."

"Smith Brothers?"

"Yeah, off the cough drops," said Ali, slapping his thigh. "No, I must be wrong; he got too much hair."

A bearded youth on a bicycle spotted Ali and rushed over, thrusting his hand through the open window. "Let me shake the hand of the only true heavyweight champion of the world."

"They made me bigger by taking my title," said Ali. "Before, the little man on the street couldn't identify with me. He'd say 'You not with me; you up on the hill with Whitey.'"

"Mr. Ali," said a black man, leaning into the car, "let me thank you for sticking up for Black America."

"There are only two kinds of men," said Ali, "those who compromise and those who take a stand."

"You are beautiful," said someone out of the crowd engulfing the car. "You ever going to fight again?"

"Yeah, I'll be doin' the Ali Shuffle again someday. Excuse me now. I need some quiet to study my speech."

He chuckled softly as Captain Jerry expertly eased the big car through the crowd, out of the Plaza, and onto a sidestreet. "I don't say we shall overcome," said Ali, "because I done overcame."

He pulled a heavy black briefcase initialed *M. A.* onto his lap. "This is my boxing gloves now," he said, opening it and riffling through books and tape spools until he found a thick sheaf of oversized white index cards on which Ali and his young Muslim bride had lettered his speech. In blue ink, written across the top card, were his opening words: "We have a serious race problem here in America."

The speech lasted twenty-five minutes. The crowd, basking in the golden sunshine, was friendly but not particularly moved. Ali's delivery, high-pitched and severe, contrasted with his firm and glowing good health. It was hard for the crowd to take him seriously when he said that he had come as a representative of Elijah Muhammad, the man who could save the country with his program for orderly racial separation.

There were very few light moments in the speech. The crowd laughed only once, when Ali said, "Now, you sport fans, when I told you a man would go in five, you put your money on it. You know I never been wrong. I missed my prediction on Sonny Liston by one round, but he was no fool, he stayed on his stool."

The crowd applauded when Ali said, "Black is beautiful," but he lost them when he said, "Now I'm gonna drop the bomb. I don't mean to offend you integrated couples,

but we believe that mixed marriages should be pro-
hibited."

The crowd lost its good nature then, and hooted and
booed, and began to drift away from the platform in the
echoing plaza.

Back in the car, C. B. Atkins, the agent, said, "You'll
have to modify the speech for such a radical audience."

"I was too strong for them; they couldn't take it," said
Ali.

"You see that naked man out there?" asked Captain
Jerry.

"Where?"

"While you was speaking he was just walking around,
buck-naked."

"I don't believe that," said Ali, looking at Minister
Majied, who just smiled and nodded.

"Buck-naked. I got a picture," said Captain Jerry.
"Man, this is California. They got love-ins out here."

"I don't know nothing about that; don't want to hear
about that," said Ali, thumbing through his speech cards.
"But I saw them walk away. I had too much strength for
them. People just can't stand the truth. They want to
hear about violence or integration, but they can't stand
the truth that can save them."

*   *   *

NEW YORK, August 7, 1969. At lunch, Ali said, "Look
around. You see people eating good, dressing good, probably living better than me. You don't have to be a boxing
champ to have a good life. That's something I just

learned the last few years. I have a pretty young wife now, and a thirteen-month-old daughter and another baby five months on the way. Hope it's a boy. Doctor says my wife can have ten. Like to have three before I go to prison. Not afraid of going to prison. Read somewhere they have ninety percent black men in prison right now. Nothing's going to happen to me in prison. But there might be riots in the country when they put me away."

He seemed relaxed and in good trim for a twenty-seven-year-old out of training and caught up in the busy pace of campus speeches, conventions, and television shows. We took our time walking over to the television studio. He enjoyed the people who stopped him on the street to shake his hand.

The show was "What's My Line?" and he was the mystery guest. *Sign in, please.* He had been on the show five years before, and the panel had guessed his identity immediately. He had just beaten Sonny Liston for the first time then. This time he said he was going to trick the panel. While a makeup man applied powder, Ali made faces at himself in the mirror and practiced his mystery-guest voice, a high piping "Yiss" and a squeaky "Neeoo."

"Hey, champ, you know what you sound like?"

Ali simpered, "I'm not a girl, I'm champ of the worl'."

But when he went out on stage, he used a gruff deep voice, saying "Nope" and "Yup." I stood backstage, watching his performance on a monitor screen, and I thought, He wants to be manly, and he wants people to know who he is, just like everyone else.

The panel did not guess his identity. It did not even come close.

We took our time strolling back to his hotel, the Hilton. The sun was warm, and people smiled at him. He said he felt good these days. He said he could handle anything that came up. His appeals of a conviction for draft evasion were not going well, he said, and he thought he would be jailed; but his case would stand as an example to the world that there were forces in America determined to keep him from spreading the truth. He said that many Americans, particularly black athletes, were saying "If they can get Ali, they sure can get me too."

We went up to his room. His key did not fit the door's lock. The hotel had locked him out of his room. He did not seem perturbed, and after a few telephone calls we went down to the hotel's credit department.

Matter-of-factly, a man behind the credit desk asked for the $53.09 in charges billed to Ali's room, and told him that in the future he would have to pay room service in cash. The assistant manager told me that Ali's credit was poor in New York hotels. Apparently, hangers-on had run up bills in his name that had never been paid.

Ali peeled off a fifty-dollar bill and a five-dollar bill. The security detective who took us back upstairs and opened the door with a special key asked for Ali's autograph.

I said, "For a lousy fifty bucks they locked you out of your room."

"This don't bother me none," he said, starting to pack for the flight home to Chicago. "Word probably got around, he's not the champ no more, he's busted, you better get your money up front. That's the way it is. When you the champ you can sign and sign and sign and sign."

*   *   *

People were always saying, *If only he hadn't gotten mixed up with the Muslims . . . If only he hadn't said: "I got no quarrel with them Vietcong" . . . If only he had gone into the army and given exhibitions . . . If only he had played the game . . . Why, he could have made millions . . . He could have been the biggest thing since—*

Sometimes people would say it to his face, and he would reply very simply, with almost magical purity, "I ain't losing nothing but gaining the world."

He would muse about it some more and then come back to boxing, because, above all, he was the greatest heavyweight boxer of his time, perhaps of all time, and this loomed larger than the sermons and the television shows and the Broadway musical and the restaurant chain and the endless litigation.

"When I'm gone, boxing be nothing again," he would say. "The fans with the cigars and the hats turned down will be there, but no more housewives and little men on the street and foreign presidents. I was the onliest boxer in history people asked questions like a senator."

VII

Before the Derby: Forward Pass
Is Restin' Easy

Two stout ladies from St. Louis, their sparse blue hair damp and limp from the heat of the noon, peered into the darkened stall. One of them said, "Hi, boy, how are you feeling today?"

When the horse didn't answer, the other lady turned to the groom, Dan Barnette, and asked, "What do you call him?"

"Forward Pass," said Barnette.

"Do you call him Forward or Pass?" asked the first lady.

"I just put 'em together. I call him Forward Pass."

"Oh, thank you," said the ladies, disappointed. They waved good-bye to the horse and trudged heavily back to their blue Chevrolet.

"Sometimes," whispered Barnette, winking and spitting simultaneously, "I call him you-big-son-of-a-bitch, but I say it sweet, and he just yawns; that's his good-humor sign."

The big horse lay down in his stall, legs gathered beneath his glossy body, his head cocked as if in rumination.

"See him in there, restin' easy; he don't give a damn how many people bettin' on him, how much money, or nuthin'," said Barnette. "Tonight when we draw the hay

and give him only grain, he'll know he'll be racin' tomorrow, but he won't know if it's an overnight or the
Kentucky Derby."

Barnette, a small, wizened, bandy-legged man with
light bright-blue eyes, began working as a groom for
Calumet Farms in 1939. In 1941, he groomed his first
Kentucky Derby winner, Whirlaway.

"Whirlie, I called him. I could go in his stall and lay
down right with him. He'd walk two or three times
around me, then lay down too. I could put my hand in
his mouth, he wouldn't bite me. Naw, I don't think about
him much no more. Like you lose your dog, you don't
keep thinking about him."

Another Calumet Farm horse, Pensive, won the Derby
in 1944, but Barnette was in the army in Europe. After
the war, Barnette came back and groomed the great
Citation, whom he called Cy.

A skinny, nervous young man, perhaps eighteen,
walked into the barn and joined us. We sat and talked
about the army, and the boy said he had been in Vietnam
only twenty-nine days when a mortar blew him up. He
had just been released after nine months in the hospital.

"I got wounded in France," said Barnette, dropping
into a cloth chair.

"Shrapnel or mortar?" asked the boy.

"Pistol. Thirty-eight caliber."

"Wow," said the boy, "that musta really tore you up.
Close combat, huh?"

"Naw," said the old man, spitting. "Accident. 'Twas
one of ours."

Barnette got up and started picking around Forward Pass' stall. "After a while, horse gets confidence in you. Gets to be a real easy job. After you get a horse under control, he won't bite you, wheel on you, savage you. Always did like the studs. Used to say 'Don't give me no more of them sourpuss fillies.'

"Yep, easy life. No, never been married, though I've acted like I was on occasions. Younger grooms comin' in now are a different breed, just want to do their work and get on out; they don't care about horses no more."

He scratched the white stubble on his shapeless jaw. "Well, hell, whole world like that. You looka those gippies, what you call them, yeah, hippies, smokin' on weeds while they're deliverin' the U. S. mail."

Barnette peered in at Forward Pass. He seemed satisfied. "He don't know what's goin' on. Whole world goin' crazy, he don't give a damn."

VIII

The Pear Says: "I am Swoboda"

This friend, an architect, went to Shea Stadium one night and sat through some of a twilight-night double-header between the New York Mets and the Houston Astros. His wife and two small children had left for a vacation in the country, he said, and he felt at loose ends this Tuesday evening. And so, without dawdling unnecessarily at the office, he arrived during the early innings of the first game, long before the lights went on and while the jets trailed black streaks across a bright powder-blue sky.

He did not notice the jets. He was busy watching Nolan Ryan's fastball begin to lose speed, and he hunched into a sitting crouch when Ron Swoboda came to bat in the bottom of the ninth inning. The Mets were trailing 3-2. There were two out. The count ran to three balls, two strikes; and the architect, as he later admitted, began knocking nonexistent dirt from spikes he wasn't wearing. It was a live and unrehearsed drama; Swoboda struck out and ended the game.

"You know," said the architect much later, over a beer, "I think this is why baseball is still the national pastime. I am Swoboda. I've tried very hard to be Fran Tarkenton or even Joe Willie Namath, but I don't even know how far back they draw their arms to pass. Some friends of

48

mine skated in a private school in Massachusetts, and they can be Bobby Orr, but not me. And as for soccer, I don't even know what the ball feels like. But I am Swoboda."

The architect rubbed his finger in the wet rings his beer glass had left on the wooden table. "Let me tell you about my greatest day in sports. I was thirteen years old and very fat. The kids in school called me The Pear. I guess they thought I was shaped like a pear.

"Well, one day about this time of year, late spring, our class was scheduled to play for the school championship, and the captain got appendicitis, and the second base-man's father pulled him out of school to take a trip, and the left fielder threw a book at the teacher. He lost his eligibility.

"I was in a small class, and there were only three substitutes on the team. I was the third. The assistant captain requested permission to field an eight-man team, and when the teacher said No, the assistant captain requested permission to play a girl. The teacher said No. So The Pear opened in right field.

"The first time I came to bat, the assistant captain, whom I did not like by this time, told me just to get a piece of the ball. I swung very hard, three times. The third time I swung, the ball was already in the catcher's mitt, the assistant captain told me.

"Things went better in the field. Only two balls were hit to right field, and the center fielder ran over and caught them both. The second time I got up, the assistant captain told me to wait the pitcher out and get a walk. I struck out, looking.

"We played seven-inning games, and the third time I got to bat was the bottom of the seventh. Two out and the bases empty. The score was 1-0, theirs. The assistant captain asked special permission to skip me in the batting order or have a girl pinch-hit. The principal was there, and he said No. The assistant captain threw his glove over the fence and cried.

"Well, the first pitch was a called strike, and the second was a ball. I could tell since it bounced before it reached the plate. I closed my eyes on the third pitch and swung from the heels and showed them where I lived. The assistant captain was screaming for me to hold up at first, but I went into second standing up. I would have been out, but the second baseman got rattled and dropped the ball.

"The leadoff batter came up, and he grounded to shortstop, an easy out; but I was running now, really steaming along, and when the first baseman saw me run, he started laughing and dropped the ball. I turned third and kept on going home.

"The assistant captain was screaming for me to go back to third, and so were both teachers and the principal and all the girls, but I just kept going. I remember very vividly seeing the catcher take the throw from the first baseman and crouch in front of the plate and grin at me and the last thing I thought was, Make way for The Pear. I think you would have had to be very fat once to understand how much I enjoyed running that catcher down.

"He wasn't able to hold on to the ball after I hit him, of course, and I scored, and the leadoff got to third. He came home on a single, and we won the game, and everyone shook my hand or kissed me. Even the assistant captain made a little speech."

The television set over the bar was dark by now; the Mets had long since lost the second game of the doubleheader 6-5. The architect, very satisfied and slightly high, got to his feet. "This sport," he said a trifle pompously, "is dull and contrived and made complicated by algebra whizzes who never measured up to their early promise. But it lives because I am Swoboda."

SUMMER

I like my job best when I'm traveling somewhere new to talk with people I've never met before. I've gotten to most states and major American cities. In 1965 I spent the summer reporting on sports in Europe, and in 1967 I went to the Soviet Union.

Sportswriters travel as much or more than any other newspaper specialists, but usually spend very little time in one place. The baseball writer is in a city for two or three days at a time, for example, and spends a great many of his waking hours getting to and from the airport, the hotel, the stadium, and the only restaurant in town that serves dinner at 1 A.M. after a night game.

The two foreign assignments offered me the added luxury of being able to spend weeks in a single city. I was also able to meet foreign sportswriters, who sounded amazingly like American sportswriters. We talked—sometimes through interpreters—about all those days and nights we spent on the road, chasing stories from town to town and hoping our luggage and stomachs would catch up.

I

A Norwegian Fishing Guide
and His River

The Laerdal River is fifty miles long, boiling out of the mountains of southwestern Norway and down into the great Sognefjord, where it meets the salmon and the sea trout fighting their way upriver to spawn. The final fourteen-mile stretch of the Laerdal is considered some of the best sport fishing in Europe, and it is said to have swallowed the lures of more dukes and princes than any other river in the world.

For most of his life Olaf Olsen has guided the rich to the pools where the trout skulk, to the swift currents that carry the salmon. He has tied dry flies for Prince Harald of Norway, just as his father did for Prince Axel of Denmark, as his grandfather did for the English lords who once controlled the river.

"I love this river; it is my life," said Olsen one summer afternoon. "I have fished all of it. The river holds no secrets from me."

He stood, small and brown and gray-haired, on the rocks along the Hunderi Pool, his favorite sea-trout beat. We watched one of his clients, a lanky Norwegian businessman, cast clumsily into the gin-clear water. The businessman had booked Olsen's services, at eleven dollars a day, and the use of the beat, at sixty-five dollars a day, more than a year ahead of time. Like most sport fishermen, he looked both uncomfortable and blissfully happy.

It was still early in the afternoon. A warm sun hung over the river, filling some of the shadows in the valley between sheer, purple-gray mountains. Twice, Olsen's client snagged his line on some bushes behind him, and each time the little guide freed it. "Ah," breathed Olsen as a brown shape moved in the water and "ah" again as the client cast out at it. The brown shape moved on, and the client grinned sheepishly.

"You must strike it exactly, precisely, hard and quick," said Olsen, "not a long pull, but sharply, just as you see him begin to disappear. It is not easy."

"Not for me, it's not easy," said the client.

"Once," said Olsen, "a great salmon came into this pool, a salmon at least seven inches longer than the largest I ever caught, which was fifty-four pounds. This salmon arrived on the seventeenth of July and stayed until the fifth of September, the day the season ended.

"He always lay in the middle of the pool. There was no difficulty reaching him. Every day I fished for him, with every kind of tackle I knew. And he just lay there and made fun of me."

"Of you?" said the client.

"Yes," said Olsen, "and he was only a salmon, who is not nearly as intelligent as a sea trout."

Smiling, the client went back on the rocks and began to cast again.

On this summer day in 1965, there were thirty fishing

rods working the famous stretch of the Laerdal. Two of the rods belonged to an English couple who had come thirteen hours by steamer from Bergen with two of their own servants. Once this would not have been worthy of notice. From 1837 to 1925 the river was fished mostly by English sportsmen who broke for tea whether the sea trout were biting or not. These men wrote books about the river that were not only records of fish caught and lost but were also rhapsodies to the mountain streams which bleed down the rocks and hurtle down the gorges to the dark little pools beneath the pines and firs, to the white and green rapids which plunge past cow and mink and potato field.

For a while an Englishman owned the river; then he sold it to a prosperous Laerdal man. In 1960, under a new Norwegian law, fishing rights became the property of the fifty-odd farmers who owned land along the banks of the river. Now there are twenty beats, or fishing areas, and fishing privileges must be leased from the farmers for at least a season at a time. The leases are further sublet for a day or a week or a month at a time. In one season, sportsmen paid more than thirty-five thousand dollars just for the right to fish in the river. They caught fifteen hundred salmon and three thousand sea trout, some of which weighed more than twenty-five pounds.

"Olsen," bellowed the client, suddenly struggling with his rod.

The guide moved quickly onto the rocks, taking the rod from his client. His stubby brown fingers danced over the rig, ripping off the fly, replacing it, untangling the reel. Then he straightened up and began to move his arm, slowly at first, and life seemed to flow from his shoulder and through his wrist and into the 8½-foot fishing rod, moving it like a whip, the green line snaking out into the water, hitting, moving, then coming back as the rod and the arm became one.

Olsen began to smile, and the client shook his head with wonder. Then Olsen stopped, as if suddenly remembering that he wasn't there to fish. He returned the rod to the client and walked back to where we had been standing, away from the rocks so our shadows would not frighten the fish.

"I am fifty-three years old," said Olsen, "and only once have I left Norway. Last year I went to Scotland to fish with a group that comes here every year. We caught fifteen salmon. I caught thirteen myself."

He lit his pipe. "But this is my river, my life. Once a Canadian came, a very rich man with a bad heart, and he lost two salmon in a row. We rested, then tried again. The salmon struck, and just as it leaped out of the water my client fell over. With one arm I caught him, with the other I fastened the rod to a fence. Then I ran for the doctor, and we took the Canadian to the hospital. He was dead.

"Two hours later I came back, and the salmon was still on the line. I played him slowly and brought him in. Often I have wondered how I thought to fasten the rod at such a time."

Such thoughts Olsen usually reserves for the long winter, most of which he spends in the basement of his neat, cozy house in the town of Laerdal. There, with his seventy-six-year-old father, his twenty-five-year-old son, and two other Laerdal *ghillies,* or guides, Olsen ties the dry flies which are sold under his name throughout Europe. From October until May it is sunless and cold in the valley of the Laerdal, and Olsen aches for the season.

"I have cold thoughts in the winter," said Olsen. It was nearly evening now, and the client had gone back to his hotel. Olsen and I were sitting in overstuffed chairs in his living room. "There are four hundred nets on the Sogne Fjord, put out by commercial fishermen. The nets trap ninety percent of the fish before they get to the Laerdal. In the winter I worry about that.

"I worry about the hydroelectric station they will build in the mountains someday. I am afraid it will slow the water and change the river. What will happen to the fish?"

He sighed and tamped fresh tobacco into his pipe. "Well, the Swedish poachers came. I chased them away. The Germans occupied our valley in the war, and I was able to convince them not to fish. Farmers put nets on the Laerdal; we got new laws to stop them. All the young men leave the town to work at an aluminum factory, but my son stays with me on the river."

The guide smiled. "But those are winter thoughts. This is the season now, the best time for me. Even with such a poor fisherman for a client, it is the best time. I can stand in the sunshine and watch the fish and look at my river."

II

Down Among the Hammer Throwers

They were waiting for Harold Connolly at the awards stand, glancing at their watches, digging their shoe tips into the stubbly grass of Randall's Island, squinting through the bright June sunlight at cars moving along the Triborough Bridge overhead.

"Maybe Connolly just went home," one of them said. "You know, this is everything to Harold."

"It's a matter of sportsmanship," said Ed Burke, the winner. "You can be an animal in the ring, that's all right, but afterwards . . ."

The third-place finisher, Tom Gage, couldn't stop smiling. A recent Cornell graduate, he had just thrown the hammer 215 feet 2 inches, the best throw of his life, good enough to put him right behind the great Harold Connolly at this championship track meet in New York City. Connolly, the veteran Olympic star, had won this event nine times in the past eleven years. But this day's throw, 218 feet 12 inches, was only good enough for second place.

"Harold will show up," someone said. "Maybe he just went to take a quick shower."

"He should be here now," said Ed Burke.

Burke was not smiling. His throw, 220 feet, was not

the best of his career, but it had been good enough to beat the great Harold Connolly. Now some of the pleasure of his victory began to drain away as he stood in the hot afternoon sun with nothing to do but wait for Harold.

It was a big day for him, Burke told those of us who asked, but he kept glancing over our shoulders for the burly figure of Connolly. Burke was twenty-six years old, a history instructor at a California junior college who had begun throwing the hammer as a student at San Jose State. He had been a discus thrower then, and the coach thought that Burke's arms were a little too short for the platter-shaped discus but just right for the hammer, a 16-pound steel ball at the end of a long wire.

Burke, a powerfully built six-footer with sun-bleached hair, switched to the hammer. The hammer was going to take him to the 1964 Olympics in Tokyo, he told a pretty blonde classmate named Shirley, who used to watch him practice the vicious twisting windups of the hammer throw and try to tell him what he was doing wrong.

They got married in Ed's junior year, and they worked on the hammer together. Sometimes Shirley would cut her own classes to attend Ed's and take notes for him so he could go to a track meet and photograph the great Harold Connolly with an 8-millimeter camera. At night they would study the films. After graduation, Shirley worked as a secretary while Ed earned a master's degree in international relations.

Ed also asked Connolly if he might practice with him. Connolly said Yes. The story gets a little fuzzy here because Connolly does not discuss it. Burke says that he asked Connolly what he was doing wrong and the older man said, "You're doing fine; everything's just fine."

"When I got to Tokyo," said Burke, his eyes still search-ing the field, "I realized that I didn't know how to throw the hammer at all. I don't want to say anything more about Connolly."

The field men compete in their own little pocket of the track world. They may hate each other; they may try to psych each other, but they can really depend only on each other for understanding. Through the long lonely hours of practice that began again for Ed Burke after his poor showing in Tokyo, he inspired himself by thinking about Connolly.

Connolly—thick-shouldered, squat, graying—a school-teacher with a perpetual half-smile, was very gracious to Burke when they met at track meets after Tokyo. But later on, as Burke's throws got closer and closer to Connolly's, the older man grew more reserved. On the day that Burke won, Connolly sat against a wire fence, like a half-smiling Buddha, watching his young rival throw. Connolly rose slowly for his own last throw of the com-petition, and when it fell short, he lumbered off the field without a backward glance.

And now we were standing in the sun, wondering if the great Harold Connolly would show up for his second-place medal. Tom Gage was thanking Burke for pointing out a little mistake he was making with his foot, and Burke was saying that he wasn't angry at Connolly any-more, that the man he would use to inspire him now was Romuald Klim, the Soviet thrower who had beaten them all in Tokyo.

"I'm going to get Klim," said Burke. "He's a boastful,

haughty, belligerent guy. Every time he wins it's a personal triumph for Leninism or something. Well, I'm going to—"

Burke fell silent, and everyone turned to follow his gaze. Moving slowly across the field, half smiling, freshly showered, and wearing a clean white shirt, was the great Harold Connolly.

Connolly reached the group and nodded to Tom Gage. "Nice going," he said.

"Tom's a real comer," said Burke brightly.

Gage, caught between the two men, shifted his feet awkwardly and said, "We'll see what happens."

Burke turned to Connolly. "How many of these have you won, Harold?"

Connolly shrugged.

Burke grinned at him. "You don't mind letting a kid have one once in a while, do you?"

III

Arnold Palmer Tees Off

At eleven o'clock one summer morning a woman in a billowing pink housedress drifted languidly out upon the terrace of her apartment in Clifton, New Jersey. She had a coffee cup in one hand, a cigarette in the other. Below her, a hundred people gathered at the first tee of the Upper Montclair Country Club's golf course, idly watching a professional from Texas tee off in the first round of the $100,000 Thunderbird tournament.

"Man, it's hot," said one of the watchers, barely interested in the Texan. "Have you seen him yet?"

"Not yet."

"Should be along any minute, shouldn't he?"

"Any time now."

Cars buzzed along the Garden State Parkway. A man sucked on his pipe, made a face, and knocked it out on his heel. It was too hot to smoke. A woman wiped away her melting makeup.

"He's coming, he's coming."

"Where?"

It sounded like the roll of drums, but it was only a stampede—hundreds, maybe thousands of spectators, skipping, jumping, running to keep up with the trim broad-shouldered man in a loose yellow shirt who signed autographs without losing a step.

"Marshals! May we have some marshals on the first tee, please?" yelled the starter as the crowd swirled outside the yellow ropes, jostling, pushing. "Please."

The woman in pink was no longer alone; two other women now flanked her on the terrace. The other terraces overlooking the golf course were suddenly alive with people, and more appeared on the apartment house roof, like crows on a telephone line.

"He looks in a bad mood," whispered a man near the yellow rope.

The crowd fell silent.

The world stood still.

Arnold Palmer had stepped to the tee.

"Wow," they roared when his ball streaked down the fairway.

"Yooooooooo," they screamed when he sank a long putt on the first.

"Ooooooooooh," they breathed when his drive sailed straight and true on the second hole.

"Get in, get in, get in," they crooned at a second-hole putt, then "no, no, no" when it rolled too far.

And finally—chuckling at each other—"Didja see him mess that one up, didja? Haw."

He was not playing very well that morning, not nearly as well as his partners, Gary Player and George Archer. But as far as the crowd that moved with them from hole to hole was concerned Arnold Palmer might have been playing alone.

Arnie's Army, Palmer's Pack. It scampers, it hops, it

runs up hills, breaking loose the instant after it explodes at the magic moment that comes but eighteen times a day —when the great man holes out. They're off, ready and waiting at the next tee, and the quick among them can press up against the yellow rope and watch him perform.

"Can you see if he's laughing?"

"I think he's still in a bad mood."

Palmer was merely smoking, dragging on the cigarette as if it held the wind's secret, frowning down at the grass, flattening it with a glance. He put on his white glove, flexing his fingers eleven times until the leather surrendered to the shape of his left hand. He stood, and Player and Archer seemed to disappear into the course. Only Palmer was there.

He rolled his shoulders under the yellow shirt, thrust out his left hip. Electric. He flipped his cigarette onto the grass and took his stance. He swung and froze, his eyes tracking the ball down the fairway. Then he curled his lip and blew some air out of the corner of his mouth. The crowd went to pieces, screamed, and started running.

Palmer picked up his smoldering cigarette, puffed, and moved on.

Cars pulled off the Garden State Parkway, and faces appeared at their windows. Women and children gathered in clumps along the slate and wire fences that separate the course from local backyards. Two state-trooper cruisers chased away the parked cars, and the troopers got out to watch. Unaccountably, a police helicopter landed outside the course, and Palmer scowled the whirling blades into silence.

"He dresses so nice," said a teen-aged girl.

"Yeah," said her friend.

"And strong, too."

IV

The Caddies Root for Murphy's Kid

"Your typical, average professional caddie is a broken guy," said Bill Manwaring, a typical, average professional caddie. "We don't have roots, don't have steady jobs. Don't even pay income tax, a lot of the guys. If I was going to do this over again, I wouldn't want to do it. It's all right for young kids. Get some money, go to college. That's why we're rooting for Murphy to win, we're rooting for Murphy's kid."

Murphy's kid was Jeff Albanese, a shy, skinny, high-school sophomore with braces on his teeth. In a month he would be fifteen years old. Because of his age and because this tournament—the $250,000 Westchester Classic in Harrison, New York—was his first professional tournament, his name had been dropped into the caddie pool for the lesser golfers. Two days before the start of the tournament, when he reported to the caddie master for his uniform, he was told he would carry the clubs of Robert Murphy, a twenty-five-year-old rookie from Nichols, Florida.

"I never heard of him," said Jeff. "He wasn't supposed to be so good."

But Murphy opened the tournament with an eight-under-par 64, held his lead the second day with a 69, and came into the final round far ahead of the field. He had needed only two hundred and one strokes for fifty-four holes—fifteen strokes under par and three strokes ahead of his nearest rival, the plodding old pro, Julius Boros. And by Murphy's side, handing him clubs, pointing out the placement of the pins, estimating the yardage, was Murphy's kid.

Caddies these days tend to be high-school and college students, particularly at professional tournaments in the summer when country clubs make an effort to enlist youngsters at the expense of the full-time touring caddies. Jeff Albanese, the eldest of nine children of a Port Chester, New York, electrical contractor, was younger than most, but otherwise he was a typical, average semi-professional caddy.

"We figured," said Manwaring, the typical, average pro, "that if Murphy wins fifty thousand dollars for first place, he'll give the kid twenty-five hundred dollars. Now that's a start toward college."

"I'd buy a car," said Jeff, who was lounging in the sun against the white wooden wall of the caddie shack.

"You're too young to drive."

"I'd save it for a couple of years."

"I'm telling you," said Manwaring, "you go to college."

At 2 P.M. Jeff hoisted Murphy's 40-pound bag of clubs onto one thin shoulder and began the four-and-a-half-hour trudge over the hilly course. To accommodate television, Murphy's threesome was the last group out, and sometimes the entire tournament was trailed by two contrasting figures: the bouncy 210-pound Murphy walking empty-handed, and the staggering 120-pound Jeff Albanese bent double under the bag and the broiling sun.

Meanwhile, up ahead, old Julius Boros, fat and crafty and persistent and impassive, shot a 33 for the first nine holes. Murphy needed an extra putt on the ninth hole, and he lost a chance to stay even with Boros. Murphy shot a 37.

"There's that kid," someone whispered as Murphy and Jeff swung into the back nine. "I read about him in the paper this morning. He's a very young kid, and he stands to make a fortune."

But old Boros came on and finished the round with a 68, which brought his total for the tournament to 272, sixteen strokes under par. Murphy came up to the last hole with a chance to beat Boros by gambling on a long shot, but he played it cagey. The crowd fell silent as Murphy prepared to putt. The hole was fifteen yards away.

If he made it, he would be tied with Boros, and they would play off. If Murphy missed the putt, he would drop into a three-way tie for second place, with Jack Nicklaus and Dan Sikes.

Jeff Albanese's thin face suddenly looked strained. The fifteen-yard putt could be worth thirty thousand dollars to Murphy and maybe as much as two thousand dollars to Murphy's kid.

Murphy missed.

After it was all over, after Boros got his check for $50,-000 and Murphy and Sikes and Nicklaus each got one for $20,416.66, I went down to the last hole and found

Jeff Albanese slumped on a wooden chair in the official's tent.

"How do you feel?"

"Not so good," he said. Then he shrugged. "I'm happy. Murphy's a good guy. He shouldn't have played it so safe on that last hole, and he had some trouble with putts, but it's okay. It's only my first pro tournament."

V

Athletes in Wheelchairs Compete
for the Paralympic Team

Joanne Keyser, the sixty-yard-dash champion, had just won the first heat in a fierce blonde blur, and now some of the girls had gathered along a sideline to discuss their chances. Linda Laury, a buxom, twenty-six-year-old redhead who had never competed before, was flip. "I didn't come to set records," she said. "I came to have fun."

Hope Chafee, a young chemist from Chicago, hefted an 8-pound practice shot, as if to assure them all that sixty-yard dashes were only an afterthought with her, that shot-putting was her game.

But Ella Cox, her long blonde hair tumbling onto her tanned, shapely arms, was clearly nervous. Keyser had broken her sixty-yard-dash record and taken her championship away a year ago, and Ella wanted it back. "What do you expect?" Ella snapped. "Keyser is all arms and young."

The sun boiled out of a pale-blue sky, making their wheelchairs hot to the touch. Volunteer officials, lithe students from Pace College and Queens College, called out names for the next heat.

Ella and Hope checked out Linda's chair. The 8-inch front casters had been tightened so the chair would stay in its lane during the race. Normally the casters are loose enough to allow the chairs to turn. The brake on Linda's chair had been removed completely for the race so she wouldn't accidentally engage it during her follow-through.

"Here goes," said Linda, still acting flip. She left her purse with Ella, shrugged theatrically, and wheeled out among the tape markers that made a wheelchair race-course from the rutted asphalt parking lot behind the Joseph Bulova School of Watchmaking in Astoria, Queens, New York.

Beyond the parking lot on a large and grassy field, the archery, discus, shot put, and javelin events of the twelfth annual national wheelchair games moved into the middle rounds. There was a sharp edge to the outdoor competition that summer of 1968, as there had been earlier in the indoor events, the swimming, table tennis, weight lifting, and bowling. Among the nearly three hundred male and female competitors from thirty states were some who had supposedly retired and others who had not been seen since the Kingston, Jamaica, Paralympic Games of 1966, or even the Tokyo Paralympic Games of 1964. Everyone who could make it was in Queens that week, competing for a spot on the American Paralympic Team that was to go to Israel in the fall.

The starter's gun snapped, and Linda got a good start. Her hands moved rhythmically on the outer steel rim of the big back wheels, in short choppy strokes that brought the chair to full speed early. The girl in Lane Two, the bad lane, foundered in a rut; two others lost strength; and Linda, pumping steadily with long coasting strokes, took the lead in the stretch and won.

Ella, who had coached her, laughed and clapped as Linda rolled back into the group. Linda was flushed, and her hands shook with excitement. She took her purse and Hope's 8-pound shot from Ella as her friends rolled out for the next heat.

Ella and Hope also qualified for the next round in Class II competition. This class is mainly for polio victims and others whose handicap places them somewhere between the incomplete quadriplegics of Class I-A, who have serious spinal damage and no abdominal support, and the "walkers" of Class III, who are too crippled to compete in normal athletics but do not necessarily need wheelchairs or crutches in normal life. Everyone in paralympic games, however, must compete from a wheelchair.

Ella Cox, the former champion, had been stricken with polio at five; Hope at eight. Both were twenty-three years old in 1968, and both felt they had had an easier time of it than red-haired Linda. Suddenly and mysteriously, one morning when she was thirteen years old, Linda was unable to rise from the breakfast table.

"Small children make adjustments and friends," said Ella, "and adults, if they don't become embittered, work hard to get their independence back. But teen-agers are just at that age when everyone is running off for a pizza, and there's a great tendency to withdraw."

"I had depressions," said Linda, "but not so much over my handicap as over where to go to meet other people like me. I had to function the best I could in an AB world."

"AB?" I asked.

"Able-bodied," said Linda.

Hope nodded and wheeled closer. "You never really know what a wheelchair can do until you see other people doing it."

The three girls met as undergraduates at the University of Illinois, which has one of the country's finest rehabilitation centers. Ella and Linda, who work for the government in social security administration, live together in an apartment, drive cars, and square dance and bowl from wheelchairs.

"If you're a good gimp, you'll do all right," said Linda.

"Gimp?"

"We like to use that word first, before an AB does."

Ella, Linda, Hope, some of the other competitors, and Ben Lipton, the director of the Bulova School and the guiding spirit behind American wheelchair games, all insist that sports for the handicapped are now more social and recreational than medical, although they were originally developed after World War II for therapeutic purposes. Now, the Vietnam War has created a large new wave of young wheelchair athletes.

Hope and Linda wheeled out again for their last heat, and Ella said, "You know, we consider this sport. We come here to win and have fun. But AB's don't really understand this. Even after you give them some big hairy explanation, it comes out sob-sister for most people. Please, one thing, don't go back and write a sob story about us."

I told her I didn't feel sad at all. She smiled, and we turned to watch the race. Hope drew the bad lane and finished fourth, wheeling back to gather her shot and try to make the team in her own event. Linda, the beginner, placed in the semifinals and wheeled back glowing.

Ella finished her racing day with a stirring second-place finish, behind the unbeatable Joanne Keyser, and then they all moved off to group around a husky hundred-yard-dash man who was leaning out of his wheelchair and saying, "Atlantic City is for old people and cripples. Now, I like Ocean City. That's for me, that's where the action is. How about you?"

VI

Casey Stengel Has a Conversation

"Respect your tools," said Joe Medwick, twisting around in the front seat of the limousine. "That's the first thing I teach 'em. You got a good bat, keep it locked up in your locker, or the pitchers'll use it and break it on you."

"The pitchers will break it on you every time," said Casey Stengel from the back seat.

"And shoes," said Medwick, flush and hearty after whiskey and steak, "shoes is very important. Kids these days don't know how to buy shoes. Shoes got to be tight. You buy shoes cheap and after a rain and a few night games, they stretch, and then you see these kids wearing four socks under their shoes. Basketball socks."

"Terrible," said Stengel. "Y'know, one time I lost a twenty-three-inning game for a pair of shoes. Had a fella on third, stole fifty-four bases the year before, and he run home in the last inning, which was the twentieth, and he stumbled two times and was out.

"So they asked him, 'Last year you stole forty-six bases, and now in the nineteenth inning you stumble two times.' And he says, 'Waal, I didn't figure Mr. Stengel was going to put me in, so I didn't wear my good shoes.' It looked like house slippers he had on. I managed four more years there, and let me tell you I never sent a pinchrunner into the game without first looking at his feet."

"And gloves," continued Medwick, pounding the seat. "I tell these kids to put their names on their gloves, and if I see a glove around loose, I take it and hide it in my locker for a few days and really let them sweat."

"You don't say," said Stengel.

"I heard someone stole Carl Erskine's watch at the party," said Edna Stengel.

"Haw!" exploded Medwick, waving the red box with his own gift watch inside. "First thing I ever learned— you never let go of anything that's got your name on it. Especially at a party."

They lapsed into brief silence. It had been a good party at Shea Stadium, a gathering of old-time Dodgers, Yankees, and Cincinnati Reds. Stengel had welcomed them as "fellows I'm glad to see ain't been buried yet," and Medwick, burstingly proud of having just been elected to the Hall of Fame, was the star of the two-inning old-timers' game played before the regular Mets' game.

Later, the old-timers trooped upstairs to drink and eat and tell stories. They laughed again at the old one about the apocryphal old-timer who was asked, "How do you think you would do in modern-day baseball?"

"I think I'd hit about three-twenty."

The interviewer then asked, "Only three-twenty?"

And the old-timer answered, "Hell, I'm seventy-five years old."

The limousine swept soundlessly on toward the city, and Mrs. Stengel pointed toward La Guardia Airport and whispered to me, "Have the planes been taking off on—"

"Quiet," said Stengel, "I'm asking this man a question. I noticed how you took two strikes and hit the ball to right field."

Medwick puffed up and pounded the seat. "I tell these kids, stupid, you can't swing for the fences, you got to learn to hit to the wrong field, these Drysdales and these Gibsons, you can't swing from down there and expect to hit them."

"We'd come to St. Louis," said Stengel, "and there you were, an hour before anybody else, taking batting practice."

"I sure did."

"I looked at a boy on the Coast, luckiest day of his life," said Stengel. "He went four-for-four and I knew we needed catchers bad, and I said, 'Yes, sir,' and they gave him seventy-five thousand. He ain't done nothin' since. I don't think he *can* do anything, and I have given up looking at prospects for one day only."

The limousine swept into Manhattan, and the driver asked, "Which hotel?"

"The Hilton," said Medwick.

Mrs. Stengel said, "And then go to the—"

"Quiet, the man is talking," said Stengel.

"One year," said Medwick, "I led the league in twelve of thirteen hitting departments, and I expected a sizable raise, and Mr. Rickey cut me by five thousand bucks. I said to him, 'How can you do this?' And he said, 'I expected you to hit three-seventy-four again.'"

"It's enough to make you an anarchist," said Stengel.

"The Essex House, please," said Mrs. Stengel.

VII

Croquet: Lawn Enough and Time

In a corner of London where there was lawn enough and time, Dudley J. V. Hamilton-Miller relit his pipe, hefted the mallet he had used since 1926, and slowly, coolly, stalked onto the playing field. He ignored the sudden rain; a croquet match is suspended only when the court is under water.

On the veranda of the Roehampton Club, in green wicker chairs, half a dozen other players watched the tall, retired headmaster neatly stroke a wooden ball through a narrow iron hoop.

"A tidy shot, Hamilton-Miller," groaned his opponent, Roger Hicks.

"Perhaps," said Captain H. G. Stoker, who had lost to Hamilton-Miller that morning, "but I have seen him play better."

They fell silent as Hamilton-Miller, his large face impassive, moved about the court, measuring the lie of the four balls with quick flicks of his blue eyes, his mind jumping three, four, ten strokes ahead.

"The end game is tensing," said Captain Stoker. "It is sheer guts; you must keep your courage going."

"Ahhh," breathed the little gallery as Hamilton-Miller's mallet struck, sending one ball across the court, the other right up to the next hoop. "That's croquet."

There are, at most, seven hundred serious croquet players in England. They pronounce it to rhyme with "smoky," and a few of them can remember the good years, like 1902, when King Edward VII sparked a renascence with his enthusiastic, if erratic, play. Many of them remember tournaments on these very same Roehampton greens when World War II antiaircraft fire rumbled in the background and to stop playing seemed something like a partial surrender to the Axis forces.

Croquet is a game of consummate skill; tactically like billiards, strategically like chess, it requires intense concentration. The ball has a diameter of 3⅝ inches, and the hoop is only 3⅞ inches wide. If a player fails to keep the four balls in carefully patterned action, he will lose his turn, and his opponent may go on to run the course and win the game.

Although Oxford and Cambridge have organized croquet teams and several British industrial firms have laid out courts for their employees, the sport suffers from its Victorian image—young ladies in wide, white dresses, blithely toeing a ball toward the hoop on the vicarage lawn when no one was looking. Croquet has also suffered from progress and democracy. A match between two people may take three hours on a rectangle of expensively manicured grass measuring 35 yards long and 28 yards wide. On that same amount of ground, without need for a gardener, dozens of people can play many other games. There are few clubs or private individuals in England who want and can afford croquet courts.

"It's really a pity," said Captain Stoker, who after eighty years could look back over distinguished careers in the Royal Navy, and Wimbledon tennis, and on the West End stage. "Croquet is a godsend in old age; it keeps the doctor at bay."

Over lunch at the club that day Hamilton-Miller had tried to explain his philosophy to me. "Games are not a preparation for life. That's nonsense, it's out of date," he had said. "Games are a part of life."

And that afternoon, his pipe failing in the rain, he was hunched over two wooden balls, swinging the mallet easily between his legs. The little gallery tensed with him.

Smack. Too hard. Stoically, Hamilton-Miller walked off the court.

"Bad luck," said Mrs. V. C. Gasson, who took up the sport after a nasty spill from a horse in India.

"Too bad," said Mrs. Gladys Riggall, who plays winters in Capetown.

"Not a wise shot," said Captain Stoker.

"And now," said Roger Hicks, who had been waiting for this moment, "ready for croquet."

"That's right," said Hamilton-Miller softly. He eased into a wicker chair as Roger Hicks struggled into his waterproofs, picked up his mallet, and strode out onto the court.

Hicks returned a moment later, dejected. He had missed his shot. The rain stopped as Hamilton-Miller stepped onto the court again for his eventual triumph. The clouds parted for the sun.

"Ah, yes," said Captain Stoker, half closing his eyes against the drifting smoke of his cigarette. "If one has to die, what better place, here on a beautiful green lawn in the sunshine—wearing clean white flannels?"

VIII

A Soviet Weight Lifter Describes
His "White Moments"

A huge man sits quietly in a small room, an almost sensual smile on his full lips as he remembers the years when every world and Olympic weight-lifting title was his, the years when he was known as the world's strongest man.

"At the peak of tremendous and victorious effort," he says in Russian, slowly and through an interpreter, "while the blood is pounding in your head, all suddenly becomes quiet within you. Everything seems clearer and whiter than ever before, as if great spotlights had been turned on.

"At that moment you have the conviction that you contain all the power in the world, that you are capable of everything, that you have wings. There is no more precious moment in life than this, and you will work very hard for years just to taste it again."

The huge man sighs. His name is Yuri Vlasov, and he is only thirty-two years old, but his best years are clearly behind him. After his great Olympic triumph in Rome in 1960, the white moments became fewer and dimmer. Now, as we talk in this small room off an air force gymnasium in Moscow in the summer of 1967, Vlasov says that winning became too easy for him, that there was not enough real competition to extend him, to prod him to greater effort.

In those years, he says, he began to look for something else. Because he had learned and seen much in "sport's speedy school of life," and because he knew he had a capacity for hard work, he decided he could make a valuable contribution through literature. In 1962, he won a short-story contest sponsored by a Soviet sports newspaper, and soon after the 1964 Olympics, in which he finished second to a younger countryman, Leonid Zhabotinsky, he left competition to write.

Trained as an air force engineer, Vlasov remained in sports as a weight-lifting coach at the Central House of the Red Army, the military sports society. But now his friends were no longer athletes, but other writers. And his heroes now were Tolstoy ("of course"), Hemingway ("how difficult it is to be brief"), Jack London ("very romantic—I know *Martin Eden* by heart"), and Guy de Maupassant ("he too wrote short stories").

Within a few years Vlasov published more than fifty stories, almost all about sportsmen. Some of them were collected in *To Surpass Himself*, a book that earned more than nine thousand rubles (ten thousand dollars) in a very short time.

"I found in sports a very rich field for writing," he says, his eyes steady and challenging behind their thick glasses. "There is tragedy, joy, and fulfillment in sports— the realization that man is master of his destiny no matter the obstacles, that faith must be based on reason and self-confidence, not on the ancient dogma of a church.

"And there is intense emotion after labor and sweat, the salty pleasure of the white moment."

But Vlasov's faith in himself as a writer began to falter. He wondered if the popularity of his work was based less on its worth than on the fame of its author. Did people think he was a freak? He pressed harder in his writing, sometimes shut up in a country cottage, away from his wife and daughter. To prove himself as a writer, he decided, he would write a semi-autobiographical novel that would explain, for all time, the essence of sport: the need of an individual to search for and accumulate strength and power. The book would gain critical acceptance, he believed, and restore his self-confidence.

But the writing went poorly. The early pages seemed artificial to him, and his greatest strength as a writer— the simple vividness of his details—was gone. Desperately he tried to re-create the white moments on paper. But he could not.

And so, in 1966, in an attempt to relieve the physical and emotional tensions building within him, he says, he returned to the weights. He thought that heavy training would restore his self-confidence. But it did not. His progress in the gym was slow and unrewarding.

"I even pity myself for coming back," he says, filling the small room with a gentle heave of his great chest. "I cannot tell people this because it would be misunderstood and considered cowardice. And now, having started, I have a moral commitment to my comrades on the team. I have to stay. Perhaps I should have thought of that before."

He clasps and unclasps his great hands, and there is silence in the room. His coach, several other Soviet lifters, my interpreter, and I stare at the bare wooden floor. We know that Vlasov's last remaining world record was broken a few weeks before by Zhabotinsky, the new strongest man in the world. We know that Vlasov has been moody since then, sometimes disappearing for a day or two at a time without even leaving a telephone number, a serious offense for a Russian officer and athlete. And we know he is training hard for the Spartakiad, the Soviet Union's internal Olympic games, scheduled for later in the summer.

The silence is broken. "Maybe I'll quit for good after the Spartakiad," says Vlasov. "I can't keep postponing my novel, my new stories forever. Sports drains my energy and leaves nothing for writing."

The great shoulders square, and the room shrinks even more. "I could beat Zhabotinsky. I could win the 1968 Olympics. But it is not worth the work."

Then the broad forehead wrinkles up to the receding hairline, and the room grows larger as the huge man sinks back in his chair. "I have to make a decision soon. I must get back to my writing. And yet, if I thought those white moments could ever return . . . Ah, but I am afraid that the pleasure is gone forever and only the salt remains."

FALL

Well-meaning people often ask sportswriters, even middle-aged sportswriters, what they are going to do when they grow up. The sports department of a newspaper is sometimes called "the toy department," and whenever a sportswriter seems to be getting a little serious, someone will take him aside and say "Take it easy, friend, it's only fun and games."

Anyone who would say that is no friend and probably not too smart either. Sports is certainly not fun and games to a halfback facing knee surgery or a gasping runner trying to break four minutes for the mile or a sportswriter who wants to cover his beat with the same intelligence and professionalism that mark the other sections of a responsible newspaper.

Politics, race, religion, money, the law—all play roles in sports. If anyone had ever doubted this, the 1968 Olympics, the so-called problem games, proved to the world that sports is no sanctuary from reality.

I

Joe Namath Is a Student of the Game

Joe Namath hunches wolfishly out of the sauna, pads across the near-empty dressing room, and roots in the thicket of fan letters, play books, film cans, and scouting reports on the top shelf of his open wooden locker. He pulls out a gift-wrapped box.

He opens the box with great interest and unfolds a pair of white cotton drawers upon which a stranger has lovingly sewn the name and insignia of the New York Jets. Namath is pleased, touched by the time and effort, but disappointed: The drawers are several sizes too wide. Someone had thought he was larger than life.

Namath shrugs, gives the drawers to the dressing-room attendant, and continues our conversation. He had said recently that most spectators don't really know what is happening at a football game. On this fall day in 1967, as he dresses after a practice session, he reconsiders his remark and decides he was right in the first place.

"I throw a pass that's intercepted," says Namath, sipping at a can of soda, "and people blame me when it was the fault of someone who wasn't where he should have been. I throw a touchdown pass, and I get the credit when it was badly thrown and only a great catch made the play."

Namath shrugs and says he is not complaining. After all, he doesn't understand nuclear physics. Today's football is getting more complex by the minute. By the time he was in high school, he says, he realized that very few people could actually follow what he was talking about.

"I can explain things to people with diagrams," he says. "Sometimes in nightclubs I'll borrow a waiter's pencil and draw it all out if it's something that's bothering me and I want to explain. But most of the time I try not to get into it too much because people just don't understand."

Namath takes down a play book and flips through it. "It's getting more and more technical every day. A defensive player might not understand something an offensive player would understand. I think most fans grasp the basics well enough, but they don't have access to the plays and films we do, and if they did, who would expect them to study as hard as we do?"

Big linemen, their faces chafed from the cold, begin straggling into the locker room after breaking into a sweat on the field. Showers hiss. A young man at the far end of the dressing room is pushing a slim booklet onto the top shelf of each locker.

"I get this a lot," says Namath, pulling on gold corduroy slacks, slipping bare feet into matching suede shoes. "A receiver is wide open, and people want to know why I didn't throw to him. Well, I've held the ball for four seconds now, and a defensive man leaves, and it looks as though there's a receiver free. But it's too late. I don't have the time anymore to go back and turn and throw to him.

"Emerson Boozer made a great run a few weeks ago, and everybody talked about it. But what about the four blocks along the way? A kicker misses, but was it his fault or the holder's, or maybe the snap from center was bad?"

The young man is about to slip a booklet onto Namath's shelf, but the quarterback sees it is from the Fellowship of Christian Athletes and shakes his head. "I won't have a chance to read it," he says.

The young man moves on, saying nothing, and Namath calls after him, "Well, I got to be honest. There's no point wasting them. They're fine things, but I just won't have the time."

II

Tips from a Man Who Eats To Win

We were sitting in a restaurant called The Elegant Farmer, in Oakland, California, and Bozo Miller, the world's champion eater, said, "The secret in my game is speed. I'm not as good as I used to be—who is?—but to beat me you almost have to kill me."

He downed his whiskey neat, and, from behind thick spectacles, morosely regarded his empty glass. He swung his arm overhead as if waving-in an airplane. When the waitress finally arrived, Bozo said, "You're not watching me, honey. You better start bringing them three at a time."

Bozo shrugged, an enormous gesture, and continued. "Now, some of these pro-football players think they're pretty good eaters. Some gamblers are trying to match me up with one of the Buffalo players, a fellow with good size. Height means nothing. I'm only about five-foot seven, down to two-seventy-five, maybe two-eighty right now, but that's a good proportion. You get one of these ballplayers, six-seven or six-eight, even one who weighs close to three hundred pounds, he doesn't have a properly stretched stomach."

The waitress returned with the drinks, and Bozo jabbed a fat forefinger at me. "My friend here is getting hungry, honey. How about eight club sandwiches?"

The waitress was new, and she blinked twice before she understood.

"Even if one of those ballplayers could handle, say, a few three-pound steaks, I'd switch to ice-cream sundaes on my turn. No athlete could handle something that rich, and if he could, I'd destroy him with hot sauces or minestrone soup. Fluids is one of my strengths."

Bozo told me he was born Edwin Abraham Miller in 1908 in San Francisco. He realized early in life that he had "a good capacity," probably inherited from his father, a circus clown and nightclub comedian, who died young of diabetes. Young Bozo would eat forty hot dogs during a nine-inning baseball game just to amuse his friends. He drifted to New York, where he worked for bookmakers and hung out with a racetrack crowd that even through the Depression had money to pay his feed bills. Mark Hellinger and Damon Runyon, two famous newspapermen of the era, would put Bozo up to such stunts as eating a small French restaurant out of all its desserts, and then they would write about it.

"That's for fun, to shake people up and give them a laugh," said Bozo. But, he said, there is no enjoyment in eating when big money rides on every bite. Bozo's most important match is said to have taken place in 1963 in the back room of a San Francisco restaurant called Trader Vic's. Bozo won the coin toss, elected chicken for easy tearing, and gulped down twenty-seven 2-pound pullets. After a while, his challenger, a Los Angeles man, licked off his fingers, sat back, and just watched his ten thousand dollars go down the drain.

Bozo said he had trained for two weeks for that match, forcing down food and fluids to the bursting point each day, gaining more than twenty-five pounds, and stretching his stomach properly.

The sandwiches arrived with three more drinks, and Bozo began to eat, very efficiently and very neatly. "Besides having self-confidence and the know-how to pick the right foods, I have fast reflexes and good coordination. Speed is all-important. Get it down fast, you destroy your opponent. Speed is more important than endurance in this game. Slow and steady is for turtles and hares. Once I had twenty-five Seven-Ups down before my opponent had eight. He got discouraged. He said, 'You're crazy,' and he walked out."

Bozo leaned across the table. "You're not eating."

Bozo's talents brought him valuable publicity in his liquor business and made him a sought-after guest at bars and restaurants in northern California. The rare nights he stayed home, he cooked gourmet dinners, which his wife and teen-aged daughters helped him serve. He claimed that no one but himself had ever been able to finish one of his meals.

He finished six of the club sandwiches and impatiently motioned me to eat up and drink down. "Let's get this stuff out of the way," said Bozo. "We've got to figure out what we want for dinner."

III

The 1968 Olympics: The Reds
and the Blacks and the Gold

In a telephone conversation one day, the president of the International Olympic Committee, Avery Brundage, said: "If we stop the Games every time there is disorder in the world, there would never be Games. At least there is one place in this troubled world free from politics, from religion, from racial prejudice . . ."

The Leader

Harry Edwards, tall and black and hard, sat on the edge of a New York hotel bed. "If there is a religion in this country," he said, "it is athletics. On Saturdays from one to six you know where you can find a substantial portion of the country: in the stadium or in front of the television set. We want to get to those people, to affect them, to wake them up to what's happening in this country because otherwise they won't care."

Edwards was twenty-five years old at the time, a sociology professor at San Jose State, a 6-foot 8-inch former discus thrower and basketball player. He had caused a national stir early in the 1967 football season when he led a protest against the housing available for black athletes. Many Negro football players, he had charged, were forced to live in motels miles from the school when there was vacant housing near the campus —but for whites only. His protest had led to the cancellation of a football game. Then he had caused an international stir with the formation of a group called the Olympic Committee for Human Rights.

"We're not just talking about boycotting the 1968 Olympics," Edwards said that night in his hotel room. "We're talking about the survival of society. What value is it to a black man to win a medal if he returns to be relegated to the hell of Harlem? And what does society gain by some Negro winning a medal while other Negroes back home are burning down the country?"

Edwards watched a plastic-tipped cigar grow cold. "I think the time is gone when the black man is going to run and jump when the white man says so, and then come back home to run and jump some more to keep from being lynched."

Bike Racer

"It starts as a game," said Jack Simes, Jr., "and then it gets to be a Frankenstein."

Jack Simes, Jr., would know. His eighty-year-old father bore scars on his head from bicycle-racing accidents, and Jack could vividly remember ending his own career in 1947 in a bloody tangle on a San Francisco track. Now we were sitting in the grandstand of a bike track in

Kissena Park, Queens, New York, watching the third generation of cycling Simeses loosen up for the 1964 national championships, a major step toward Olympic qualification.

"The trouble with coaching your own son," said Jack Simes, Jr., who was fifty, "is fear. For Jackie, the butterflies end when the race starts. For me, they just begin. I know what can happen to him."

He leaned forward, his eyes moving over the quarter-mile asphalt track until he picked out his son, a small, compactly built twenty-one-year-old with reddish-blond hair crouched over the handlebars of a two-hundred-and-seventy-dollar custom-built bike.

"His mother can't watch him anymore; she gets sick to her stomach," said Jack Simes, Jr. "Sprinting, you fall off a bike and it's like falling out of an automobile going fifty miles an hour and all you're wearing is a bathing suit."

Jack Simes III had broken his shoulder three times and smashed his nose. His legs were marked by old scars. Two years before, in Copenhagen, he had fractured his skull. He had been offered professional contracts in Europe, where a top sprint-cyclist can earn as much as fifty thousand dollars a year. But he had decided to remain an amateur and compete in the Olympics.

"The boy is always thinking," said Jack Simes, Jr., tense as his son jockeyed for position on his frail, 15-pound bike, letting the pacesetter break the wind for him.

"It's about fifty percent tactics, fifty percent muscle. You have to know your opponents' weaknesses, their strong points. Can you afford to let him get ahead to break the wind? Will you be able to catch up? What about his jump?"

Simes leaned forward as the riders edged into the curve, measured their opponents, then jumped—that moment when the rider stands in the saddle and explodes into final speed. As they hit the stretch, young Simes was fourth.

"Never make it now, not quite," muttered the father, trying not to look at the track. But his eyes kept flicking back as his son's thighs bunched, his back strained, his wrists grew thick from effort.

Suddenly young Simes swept past the field, stood up like a jockey, leaned forward, and slowed down by putting a gloved hand on the exposed front wheel.

Simes sighed and turned to me, grinning. "My daughter wanted to be a bike racer too, but I blew the whistle on that, I sure did."

Kalamazoo

Steve Mokone, the first black African to play major league soccer in England, was born in Johannesburg, the son of a cab driver. He remembers playing a great deal of soccer, barefoot—first kicking bound rags, then a worn tennis ball. He sat in a wooden chair one day and remembered, with some reluctance, the feeling of his South African youth.

"I remember most," he said softly, "the pettiness and

the insults and the brutal kinds of feelings you have when someone throws ink on your new white shirt, or pushes you off the sidewalk, or walks off without paying you for caddying eighteen holes of golf. Or a policeman shoves cigarette butts up your nose and there is nothing you can do about it; there is no recourse because you are black."

When Mokone was fourteen years old, his family moved to Pretoria. He became a star of the Sunday black leagues and a matriculated college student. The full force of South Africa's repressive control had not yet dropped upon the nonwhites, and many of them still lived in the major cities. So it was possible, by an accident, for Mokone to break free.

One Saturday, while sight-seeing, the coach of a touring British team, Wolverhampton, saw Mokone working out. They talked. The coach returned on Sunday to watch Mokone play and offered him a professional contract.

Mokone's mother insisted that he continue school. But British correspondents touring with the Wolverhampton team filed such long and glorious dispatches about the barefoot discovery that many other offers followed. A year later, at eighteen, Mokone went to Coventry, England, lured by the promise of more playing time and experience with a third-division club. It was a mistake, he says now; he should have accepted a contract with a better club. But it eventually worked out. He was very popular, a great novelty in England, although the first few months were very difficult. He had to learn to play in soccer shoes and to overcome his fear of bodily contact with white men.

"There was a lot to learn," said Mokone. "One day my landlady rushed in, excited. She said she had found me a 'homeboy.' It turned out he was from Ghana, and she couldn't understand why we didn't know each other.

"I had a friend who always got into fights when we went to the pubs. He was Irish, and he told me he was getting back at the Englishmen who had discriminated against his people. And I had thought white men discriminated only against black men."

In 1958, after three seasons, Mokone made his first trip home. It was very hard now to hear white men refer to his mother as a "jane," to slip back into the accommodating postures, to be a boy after having been a man. Although he was a great hero among black South Africans, who all knew that he had been bought by the first-division team in Amsterdam, The Netherlands, and that he was nicknamed Kalamazoo after a song of that time, he was still unknown among white South Africans.

His success, said Mokone, looking back, was a threat to the concept of white supremacy. During his trip home he had been routinely arrested on pass violations and roughed up. Mokone went on to play for clubs in Cardiff, Wales; Marseilles, France; and Turin, Italy; but he returned to South Africa only once more, in 1962. Two years later he ended his career, and in 1965, he came to the United States to complete his education.

When I met him, he was a thirty-year-old student at the University of Rochester, with a wife and a small daughter, and the beginnings of a paunch even his vest could not hide. He was in New York, speaking to anyone who would listen about the hypocrisy of allowing South Africa to participate in the 1968 Olympic Games.

"I cannot understand why they give this kind of pref-
erential treatment to South Africa, to allow her to break
the Olympic Constitution," said Mokone. "The black man
will not be allowed to participate in fair trials with the
whites for places on the team. There is great athletic
talent in the black townships, but the white man will
never see it."

Mokone's voice dropped. "I have been in contact with
many black athletes, and they are bitter about this decision. And those blacks who want to go to the Olympics
are frightened that when they defect in Mexico City,
the United States will refuse them political asylum and
they will have no place to live."

The Swordsman

"The true saber fencer," sneered an old épée man at
the Olympic trials, "spends at least one year in acting
school." As if on cue, the national saber champion, Jack
Keane, screamed, wrenched up his mask, and whipped
his blade against the copper fencing strip as his eyes
rolled toward the ceiling of the gym. "Nice, but a minor
performance," said the old épée man coolly. "You should
see his crucifixion scene. Superb."

Keane, a dark and mercurial man, lost the bout in an
upset and stalked to a corner, a titan nibbled to death by
geese. "I am a sophisticated fencer," he said through
closed teeth, "and I am being judged by men too in-

experienced to see my subtle moves—zap, zap, zap—to the wrist. Three times, and they never saw it."

Keane glowered burningly, since all saber men must constantly try to intimidate the officials, intimidate each other, intimidate the fates that will eventually clog their synapses and turn their legs to lead. While foil fencers and épée fencers are electrically judged by flashing lights and buzzers, the saber fencer is judged by men—whose eyes may be slower than his blade.

Saber fencing is not as easy to follow as the clear, straight thrusting of the épée or the controlled flurries of the foil. The saber is a bold weapon, descended from the cavalry sword, and a touch can be scored by slashing or banging or sticking or slicing to any part of the head or upper body. Saber fencing can become very emotional and saber fencers tend to posture like bullfighters and tenors.

The tension was obvious on the day of the Olympic trials in Teaneck, New Jersey. The saber fencers came into the tournament with points accrued from regional and national competitions throughout the year, but a poor showing could keep even a star like Keane off the team.

"I feel horrible, miserable, *aaaargh*," Keane had said early in the morning, flashing his great white smile, tossing his crisp black curls. As creative director on the Nixon-for-President advertising account, Keane had had little time to rest or practice recently, he said.

It was going to be a very hard day for Keane. First, as often happens in fencing matches, the four judges help-

ing the bout director were other fencers either waiting
their turns or already eliminated. Whether or not some of
them were too inexperienced to see Keane's "subtle
moves," they were all suspected of being secretly hostile:
Saber men, not always without justification, are para-
noid. By the final round, the fencers, acting in rare con-
cert, were boycotting certain officials.

Second, Keane's bounding style—his saber held arro-
gantly low as he peacocks along the strip—nearly im-
paled him on a spike left carelessly sticking out of a
wooden post in the small Fairleigh Dickinson University
gym. As he twisted and jerked in agony, clutching his
spine, spectators covered their eyes and other fencers
raised their eyebrows.

Third, Keane was tired. His strength has always been
in his determination and fierce combativeness. While
other fencers may vary the tempo of their game to press
and relax alternately, Keane never lets up. But this day
he was wearing down, and the tight skin around his jaw
had begun to sag. He looked his forty years.

But Keane hung in grimly, shrieking, and who was to
say that his intimidations didn't help. One young judge
cried, "It was good, it was good, Jack; believe me, I heard
it hit you." And Alex Orban, the great instinctive fencer,
snarled at the judge, "Be positive."

"I just want to make the team," Keane kept saying, and
naturally he ended the regular final round in a tie for
first place with Orban, who is ten years younger. Keane
lost, and flashed his dazzling smile and tossed his now
soggy curls and congratulated everyone who, like him,

was going to Mexico City, stopping only now and then to touch his spine or grit his teeth or check to see if his heart was still beating.

The old épée man, disinterested, nodded his head at me. "I'll tell you all you need to know about fencers," he said. "When General Maxwell Taylor discontinued varsity fencing at West Point, a delegation of fencers from the New York area went up to complain. After all, the sword is a military weapon. Maxwell Taylor looked at them and said, 'Frankly, gentlemen, it's the cost.'

"Well, everyone laughed. After all, what was six thousand or so dollars a year to the army. So Maxwell Taylor said, 'Frankly, gentlemen, it's the lack of facilities.'

"Well, everyone laughed. After all, West Point had the best fencing room in the country; it had been built into the original structure. So finally Maxwell Taylor said, 'Gentlemen, fencing is a sport for intellectuals, and we don't want intellectuals in the army.'"

The Party Line

A year earlier, in Moscow, a Soviet sports official had told me, "When we see Leonid Zhabotinsky break another weight-lifting record we do not say 'Aha, a clear-cut victory over capitalism.' That is foolish. It is not sport. But we must realize that his feat cannot exist outside of space and time, and it is the product of a particular society with a particular culture.

"There must be some interrelation between Zhabotinsky's feat and the advantages of a socialistic system that gives possibilities to workers, students, and peasants to practice sport and go to the Olympic Games."

Parade

And it finally came to pass. On a cloudy, mild Saturday in October, a tall and tawny Mexican hurdler moved lithely up ninety carpeted steps to the rim of a rock-hewn stadium, turned slowly to present her torch to the world, then plunged it into a stainless steel saucer and fired the flame that would burn through the Games of the nineteenth Olympiad.

There were about one hundred thousand of us in the Olympic stadium. Most were upper-class Mexicans who could afford as much as twenty dollars a ticket. Many were tourists and journalists who had started their day early to reach the great new stadium that seemed to flow from the gray stone as if it had been roughly scooped out by the hand of a god.

We had come from the heart of the city in buses and cars, along handsome, sweeping freeways that knifed through green belts and through adobe shanty towns that had been hastily, pathetically, splashed with white and red and pink and blue paint for the Games.

I remember staring through the tinted windows of the bus at dark Indian faces watching without expression. Donkeys and ragged dogs scrounged by the roadside, where small children and women with babies swaddled to their breasts picked their way among piles of refuse and stone. A man stood, balanced on a home-made wooden leg, in the cindery courtyard of his shack, distractedly kicking at a soccer ball.

Now, inside the stadium, Avery Brundage, eighty-one years old, was reading a speech in Spanish. The beautiful legions of the world were massed about him: Senegalese so black their skin seemed blue and Swedes with corn-silk hair; well-dressed throngs from the United States and the Soviet Union and Japan and Germany; and four men, in suits that did not match, from poor, corrupt little Haiti. The crowd was especially warm toward the contingent from Czechoslovakia, for that country had just been overrun by Soviet tanks. And the pride and joy in the Mexican marchers seemed to contrast oddly with the underground news photos we had seen of the Mexican student protesters who had been machine-gunned in the streets only a few weeks before.

The ceremony was very beautiful and moving, doves whirling into the air and the symbolic passing of flags. Brundage stood ramrod-straight. There were no South Africans in the Olympics—he had compromised on that —but here we all were, 7,350 feet above the level of the sea, watching a flame fed by gas burn evenly against a pale-blue sky.

The Girls

The first day of competition was a tough one for the American women's volleyball team. The girls ate early— a large breakfast because their team manager, Dr. Marie

Liba, insisted upon it—and then straggled out into the bright sunshine that gleamed off the windows and bricks of Olympic Village. The thirteen of them were living in five small rooms, with three bathrooms. It was Sunday, and six of the girls attended early Catholic Mass. The usual morning crush in the bathrooms was lessened. It was the best thing that happened all day.

The girls, most of them lanky blondes in their twenties, were quiet on the bus trip out to the Olympic gymnasium, leafing through the color spreads in the Mexican newspapers, of the previous day's opening ceremony. Several complained mildly and routinely about the inadequate laundry room, about the lack of a place to dance at the Village, and about how hard they worked for their coach, Harlan Cohen. A 2-mile run in under sixteen minutes every day, one hundred sit-ups—imagine! Volleyball is getting to be a young girl's game, they said.

I was sitting next to Barbara Perry, a tall, dark, jolly girl from Honolulu. "It's really rough playing the Jappies right off," she said. "We don't expect to win, just be respectable. What makes it tough is that we play Czecho-slovakia tomorrow, and we might beat them if we have some rest and confidence."

Coach Cohen, a tough little bachelor schoolteacher from Los Angeles, herded the girls into a warm-up room off the main arena as soon as we reached the gym. I found myself talking with Dr. Liba, a slim, middle-aged blonde. "We've got good girls," she said, "they don't smoke or drink, no discipline problems. Of course, I've insisted we all live together, so no one can sneak in after the ten o'clock curfew. Not that they would, anyway. Tomorrow night—after Czechoslovakia—I'll let them stay out until midnight."

The match between the American and Japanese girls began with all the music and marches and exchanges of gifts that make international competition so ceremonial and entertaining. All the Japanese girls were taller than the average Japanese woman, but considerably smaller than the American girls. They had been formed into a team six years before by a legendary fanatical coach named Hirofumi Diamatsu, who had them all working at one factory, living together, spending all their free hours on the hardwood floors. The crowd cheered the Japanese and casually booed the Americans. I asked an Olympic press aide, an Argentine, if the booing was part of the anti-American feeling we had noticed during the opening parade. He said No, it was just the crowd letting the American girls know that it had already seen them play.

The match lasted fifty-two minutes, and the scores were 15-6, 15-2, 15-2. Women's volleyball is usually a highly emotional game. There is a great deal of screaming and hand-clapping and shouted instructions as the girls tumble and slide and jump. But the Americans lost their zip early—it was very hard to keep spiking when a solid wall of orange-suited ladies kept rising up to bat the ball back into their faces. And it was very hard to keep diving for balls that the Japanese girls scientifically slammed just a few inches from outstretched American fingers.

The Japanese volleyball girls are one of the true and pure joys of modern sport, a team of six bodies so well trained that head or chest or stomach can return a ball as well as closed fist. The Japanese women's breasts were bound with elastic, to give them greater mobility. Yet there was nothing mechanical about the spring in their legs or the quick chatter in the back court or the joyful squeals when they won.

The bus back to Olympic Village was even quieter. Coach Cohen said his girls had never played so well, and he thought they'd do better when they became more accustomed to playing together.

"This is nothing," said Barbara Perry. "There'll be real pressure later on when we play teams we think we have a chance to beat."

The Vietnamese

"Our biggest problem is morale," said Phan Nhu My with a sad smile. "We must constantly repeat the Olympic slogan to the team: It is more important to compete than to win. We remind them how much more fortunate they are than thousands of Vietnamese back home. Sometimes it helps."

The two cyclists on the Republic of South Vietnam team came to Mexico City with virtually no special training for the high altitude there. The two girl swimmers trained in Paris, Tokyo, and Singapore on their fathers' money. The entrant in the decathlon preferred to work out when no one was around to laugh at him. The fencer was eliminated early—as most Vietnamese athletes have been since 1952, the first and last time they came as a national team representing the North and South.

"We do not have a great tradition in sports," admitted My, editor of the Vietnam Press Agency, secretary of his country's Olympic committee and chief of its mission at the Games. "When the French came to our country, they imported the European sports—cycling, tennis, football, rowing. We have a little wrestling art of our own, and some boxing, like Thai boxing. We allow kicking, bare knuckles, and elbowing."

We were sitting in a small interview room in the administration building of Olympic Village. My was chain-smoking. "The president and the prime minister agreed that we have to be here," he said, "to show the world that even a country at war is trying to normalize its life."

With their presence planned as a political gesture, the Vietnamese had begun preparing for the 1968 Olympics only in mid-1967. The government allocated five million piasters (about $42,500) for the team. Selection was not difficult: Virtually all Vietnamese athletes were either in American universities or living in Saigon.

Of the ten-member team, the three shooters were Saigon policemen, the two track-and-field men were students at San Fernando Valley State College in California, and the fencer, an army major, had recently returned from Texas State. The two girls—daughters of a doctor and a ship-owner—had learned to swim in the

30-meter pool of the exclusive Cercle Sportif Saigonnais; to prepare for competition at the 50-meter Olympic distance, the girls had been sent abroad.

Of the two cyclists, one was a soldier, the other a seventeen-year-old boy soon to be conscripted, according to My. Once quite popular, competition cycling has never been the same since the Tour de Vietnam was cancelled in 1963 when the government could no longer assure security on the roads.

South Vietnam has won a few medals in the Southeast Asia Games from time to time, particularly with its fine teams in volleyball, table tennis, and soccer, the national sport. But despite coaching and equipment from the American military, sports training remains out of reach for most Vietnamese. There is, for example, a well-equipped rowing organization, but the wealthy Vietnamese businessmen who belong to the club row only for pleasure and have no interest in training young oarsmen or scullers.

Preparation for the Olympics was halted for five months by the Tet offensive of January, 1968, and then the allocation was cut in half. Phan Nhu My said that even with the five million piasters originally promised there had been no thought of bringing more athletes or even of better training for the ones they had. The additional money would have gone for "public relations."

"In my room at the Village," he said, "are many books and pamphlets and souvenirs from other countries, telling their stories. If we had more money, we would have printed many such books, and we would have given receptions and offered entertainments."

The Vietnamese sportsmen had been apprehensive about coming to Mexico, a country they knew only from American western movies. But they were delighted by the ovation they received when they marched into the Olympic stadium on opening day, and they were charmed by the sympathy and kindness of the Mexicans.

Patiently they explained to the Mexicans that they were from the south of their country, and that only the 1952 team had represented the entire country. To his relief, said Phan Nhu My, the Mexicans seemed to show no particular favoritism toward either South or North Vietnam.

Another bright spot, according to My, has been the continuing friendship of other Asian countries. The day before My and I met, the Filipinos, Thais, Koreans, Malaysians, and Vietnamese formed a mutual defense pact for the 196-kilometer road race. It was felt that an Asian cycling alliance was necessary to offset the traditional agreements among the European racers.

The greatest frustration, My said, was trying to overcome the "inferiority complexes" of the athletes. After lengthy "negotiations," the coach persuaded the decathlon man to train with athletes from other countries. But then he insisted upon placing the pole vault bar considerably higher than the 11½ feet which was his limit.

The athlete explained that he would be humiliated if the other athletes knew that he could vault no higher than 11½ feet. He would rather keep knocking the bar off, giving the impression he was just having a bad day.

"We made him to understand," said My, "that we are not here to win, or even do well, but to learn and give our most. Then if the situation comes to a normal state, if peace should come at the end of this year or next year, we will be ready to make rapid progress in sports and take our place among the other nations of Asia."

Black Power

In the evening of the fourth day of competition, Tommie Smith and John Carlos lowered their heads and raised their black-gloved fists as "The Star-Spangled Banner" was played to celebrate Smith's victory in the 200-meter race. I thought at the time it was a pretty mild gesture for two black athletes who were students at San Jose State, Harry Edwards' school.

Zhabo

Leonid Zhabotinsky is suffering. Great waves of pain flow from his massive body, flooding the dim, warm theater. If Leonid Zhabotinsky lives through this afternoon, it will be a miracle. Slowly he works his feet into the wooden platform in the center of the stage, giving them time to take root. His mouth forms a huge O, silently screaming. He takes a great breath, sucking all the oxygen from the room.

We sit hushed, hypnotized by this 358-pound man gleaming under the hot television lights. We watch him tighten the wide leather belt until the stupendous stomach is sliced in two. We hold our breath as the man folds into a red-and-green mound, then rises slowly upward with two hundred kilos (440 pounds) in his hands —a new Olympic record for the press.

We cheer, but Zhabotinsky will have none of it. What price a record when a man is a meter from his grave? On the way offstage, he touches his left knee, obviously separated; he places a tender hand on his right arm, obviously hanging by a thread to his ruined shoulder, and in a masterstroke, almost out of sight, he lays a hand on the curve of his back. There is no question that every disc is fused. We understand perfectly and roar with laughter.

"Ah, that Zhabo," says a Dutchman sitting beside me, "he has never felt better in his life."

Not everyone is amused. Eight other heavyweight lifters have reached this final afternoon of competition, and all week they have heard rumors that gave them false hope. It was said that Zhabotinsky was ailing in the high altitude, that the Russians had asked that five minutes be allowed between consecutive lifts instead of the usual three so their star could catch his breath.

But now it seemed as if the rumors were merely the latest of Zhabotinsky's tricks. After all, so the story went, hadn't Zhabo convinced his own teammate at the 1964 Olympics, the sensitive Yuri Vlasov, that his back was sprained? Vlasov had believed Zhabotinsky, altered his tactics, and watched most of his world's records broken. Poor Vlasov had made one more attempt to recapture his title as world's strongest man and had failed. He had not even made the 1968 Soviet Olympic team.

Weight lifting is considered part brute strength, part technique, and part tactics that are often psychological. Throughout the opening-day parade, Zhabotinsky had carried the Soviet flag in one outstretched hand, a bit of psychological warfare, says the Dutchman sitting beside me, that seriously affected all the other lifters. Now, with his pretensions of injury, Zhabo was merely painting the lily—everyone knew he would win. We were interested in what new tricks the great Zhabo had for us and who would finish second and third.

There were two other contenders that afternoon, Serge Reding, a baldish, fussy-mouthed, 274-pound Belgian, and Joe Dube, a 315-pounder from Doctor's Inlet, Florida.

We sat through three events—the press, the snatch, and the clean-and-jerk. Each man was allowed three lifts in each event, and he was judged on form as well as on his ability to lift the weight in the prescribed time. Success or failure depends greatly on the amount of weight he opts to lift. The Dutchman explained to me that the rule of thumb for the three lifts is this: On the first, lift what you *can*; on the second, what you *should*; on the third, what you *hope*.

Reding, the Belgian, was cautious, raising lesser weights on his first lifts to be sure to qualify. Dube, a round-faced twenty-four-year-old, was sometimes reckless, lifting high in his determination to be the only American to win a medal in weight lifting this year. And Zhabotinsky was in a class by himself.

Zhabo came out for the snatch, staring straight ahead,

his golden-tipped curly hair glistening atop the mushy, mobile face that seemed to munch on itself—now sly, now terrified, always about to fall apart like raw marble beneath the chisel of a clumsy sculptor.

"Up, up, upupupupup," he bellowed as he snatched 374 pounds, a new Olympic record. He lowered the bar and waited on the platform for a coach to come out and rub his thighs back to life. Then he limped heavily off-stage to thunderous applause.

He lifted only once in the jerk, 456.5 pounds, twenty-two pounds lower than his jerk record, but enough to give him a total of 1,259.5 pounds and tie his total record. This time, two coaches had to lead him offstage and both were laughing. Zhabotinsky's face had fallen apart, into a wondrous wide and sunny smile that flooded the theater as surely as had his suffering and included us all in the joke.

Afterward, backstage, Reding was smiling and flutter-ing like a schoolgirl. He had won the silver. He and Dube had both lifted a total of 1,221 pounds, but the Belgian was lighter in body weight. Dube, who had won the bronze, was complaining mildly that the food here was "all right, but not like the food I eat down South," and Dube's blonde wife was waving away questions about future competitions with a "He's all mine now."

And Zhabotinsky was presiding, the host, pouring some Coca-Cola for Dube, allowing Reding to bask in his smile. "No," said Zhabotinsky, answering the ques-tions of journalists, "there are no frontiers in weight lifting."

"Why," someone asked, "didn't you try to break your own record instead of tying it?"

The great face crumbled, reassembled; the shoulders shrugged like twin volcanoes.

"What for?" he asked, smiling, and for no reason at all, he touched his shoulder, rubbed his knee, thumped his stomach, and stroked his face. Amazingly, he was still all there.

Winners

Jack Simes III, the third generation of cycling Simeses, did not win a medal in the 1968 Olympics. Nor did Jack Keane, the histrionic saber fencer. There were no medals for the hammer-throwing rivals, Harold Connolly and Ed Burke; and Klim, the Soviet athlete that Burke wanted to beat, was beaten himself and finished second. There were no medals for the Vietnamese or for the American girls' volleyball team, or, for that matter, for most of the thousands of athletes who came to Mexico City. And for most of them, returning home without medals was not a crushing disappointment—having been there, having competed against the best in the world, was medal enough.

View from the Top

"From the standpoint of our image in the world, our way of life, the Olympics was a success," said Douglas F.

Roby, the president of the United States Olympic Committee.

We were talking on the telephone. I asked him about the United States Olympic Committee's suspension of Smith and Carlos after they had raised their fists and lowered their heads.

"We suppressed the demonstrators," said Roby, "because we felt if we let it go, it would get progressively worse, it would become a tip-off to others, white as well as black. We let a lot of little things go by—berets, black socks, hands up and down—even though there are specific rules against changes in uniform in the competitor's handbook. But we felt that would be flyspecking.

"But we couldn't let a flagrant demonstration go by. We considered that we might have a boycott on our hands, but we had to take the chance."

The following day, according to Roby, he wanted to be sure that all athletes knew of the committee's decision, so he aproached Lee Evans, Larry James, and Ron Freeman as the three black athletes were preparing for the 400-meter run.

"Now, boys," he said he told them, "I don't want to upset you, but . . ."

In stony silence the three listened to Roby warn them that "any further demonstration would be dealt with to the full extent of the United States Olympic Committee's powers." Then they went out and swept the event, finishing one, two, and three and arriving at the victory stand in black socks and black berets. They raised their fists in the Black Power gesture.

"My talk spurred them on," chuckled Roby. He added

that the berets were acceptable because it was raining and because they removed them during the anthem. The raised, clenched fists were lowered during the anthem. Besides, said Roby, the raised fist was just a traditional athletic gesture of triumph that he remembered from his own playing days at the University of Michigan and with Cleveland in the National Football League.

Roby was seventy, the retired board chairman of a Detroit company that manufactured automobile parts. He said that the two problems he faced during the 1968 Olympics—the generation gap and the black-white confrontation—would be ameliorated with time. When today's young people get to be "thirty or thirty-five, they'll look back and see how foolish they were," he added.

He was rather disturbed, however, by the behavior of the all-white Harvard heavyweight crew. After they were selected to represent the United States in the Olympics, six of the nine crew members issued a statement supporting Harry Edwards' Olympic Project for Human Rights.

Later the rowers circulated a letter asking other white athletes to consider the inequality in America and the possibility of using the Games as a stage for nonviolent protest.

On the telephone that day, Roby said "they defied us" by "embarking on a social justice and civil-rights program" instead of concentrating on their rowing, "especially after we had spent fourteen thousand dollars to ship their shells and equipment down to Mexico."

I asked him if he was glad that the Harvard crew had lost.

"I won't say I'm glad they lost," said Roby. "I was terribly disappointed. But it verified my feeling that you can't head out on one project and expect to do well in another."

Aftermath

"The Games were a success," said Harry Edwards, "because the demonstration proved to all athletes that there's more to being a nigger than the color of a man's skin. If Smith and Carlos could be treated like that by Olympic officials, so could any athlete.

"Yes, I'd say it was a very successful Olympics. A foundation was laid for athletes and fans to become more involved. It was all nonviolent, no fire-bombing, and no one got stomped.

"Were there historic milestones? I don't know, but we turned over some rocks and saw what was underneath."

To Be Continued

Early in 1969, there was squib in the newspapers announcing that Avery Brundage had arrived safely in Munich to inspect the site of the 1972 Games.

WINTER

Writing under deadline is often exhilarating, and if you're lucky and the event has moved you, a rhythm develops and the story just flows out of the typewriter. This happens in boxing, in tennis, in auto, horse, and crew racing more than in most sports because the action is centralized and fairly simple. Football, baseball, and basketball are more difficult because along with most of the same deadline pressures come the complicated statistics and constant player substitutions.

I never wrote so many stories so fast as during the four years that boxing was my beat. A fight might be over at 11:15 P.M. on a night when all the copy had to be in the *Times*' office by 11:30 if it was to make the next morning's paper. Actually this was easier than it sounds. After I typed each paragraph, I would tear it out of the typewriter and hand it to the Western Union telegrapher sitting next to me at ringside, who would punch it out over a direct line to a similar machine and operator in the *Times*' sports department office. This worked whether I was just seven blocks away in the old Madison Square Garden or in the Astrodome in Houston, Texas.

Getting the story to the office is sometimes more difficult than gathering the facts or shaping them into a

coherent piece. But with modern communication sys-
tems, the problem is usually just a matter of time. At
night in a chilly arena, with the clock moving toward the
deadline, that moment comes when even the best story
in the world, finished too late, is worthless.

I

The Racetrack Subway Goes
Nowhere and Back

The fare to Aqueduct Racetrack is seventy-five cents
on the special subway train from Times Square. This
includes a send-off: The narrow escalator down to the
platform ends beneath the words *Good Luck* printed
overhead on the grimy gold arch of a huge wooden
horseshoe. The subway car is as silent as the reading
room of a library, and, in fact, all the travelers are reading, studying the charts of past performances of all the
horses that will race on this cold, hard, dreary day at the
butt end of the year.

They are very ordinary-looking men and a few women,
a bit older and shabbier than most people these days, and
they hardly move for thirty minutes as the train rockets
through the black hole of the subway, then bursts out
onto an elevated track that winds above the two-family
row houses and cemeteries of Queens. As the train finally
slides into the station they are on their feet. As it skids
to a stop they are moving to the door, and then they are
running down the ramp toward the two-dollar grandstand entrances, then on to the daily-double windows,
five minutes away from closing.

Before the first race of the day at any track, anywhere,
there is a sense of happening, of a corner that might be

turned, a door that might open. There is almost a merry ring to the pari-mutuel machines punching out fresh tickets to everywhere, and the players move out smartly, clapping down the wooden seats of chairs, briskly stepping onto the pebbled concrete areas that bear the remarkable signs *No Chairs Permitted on Lawn.* Seconds after noon the first race starts. It lasts little more than a minute, just long enough to hold your breath, to scream, or to fall to your knees against a metal fence and pray.

And then it is suddenly quiet again. The race is over, and the day is no longer fresh and new; the day is tired and old and familiar. An old, hooded maintenance man shuffles over the asphalt, picking up torn tickets with a nail-tipped stick, tapping like a blind man among the empty wastebaskets. Men watch him to see if he is turning over the tickets, looking for a winner thrown away by mistake. He is not.

The racetrack settles into a predictable rhythm. In the half hour between races, men study their charts, bundled against the chill or bent over stale coffee in the drab cafeteria or hunkered down beneath the hot-air ceiling vents in the cavernous men's room, the warmest spot at Aqueduct. As the minutes move toward post time they gather beneath the approximate-odds board. They try to interpret the flickering numbers—smart money moving, perhaps the making of a coup. At the last moment they bet, then rush out onto the stone lawn to watch the race. A minute later they are straggling back, most of them losers.

There are ebbs and flows throughout the day. People

leave, others come; the machines jangle on. There is a great deal of shuffling in the grandstand area and very little loud talk. People move away from strangers. When men speak of horses, they use numbers, not names, and when they talk about jockeys they frequently curse.

The day ends, pale and chilly, a few minutes before 4 P.M., and they troop out to the subway station. There is no special return train: The city will get you out to the track fast enough, but you can find your own way home.

Horse-players are smart, and so they all wait in the enclosed area near the change booths, ready to bolt through the turnstiles onto the outdoor platform when the train comes and not a moment sooner. They stamp their feet, listening for the far-off rumble of the train and muttering about the crooked jockeys, the cowardly horses, the heartless owners, the ugly track, the greedy state that takes ten cents of each dollar bet.

Suddenly one of them bolts. They're off, quick and practiced, tokens into the turnstile slots, bodies spinning out onto the platform. But there is no train yet; they all followed a fool, and now they curse him for five minutes in the cold until an old shuddering train lumbers in to carry them away.

II

Jake the Snake Is Hot on Ice

Jake the Snake loves his work. Three nights a week he crouches in front of a hockey goal, loose and agile on skinny steel blades, peering down the ice through the eye-slits of a plastic mask. He seems to say "I am Jacques Plante, the greatest goalie in the business, and I dare you to get one past me."

And of course they try, bursting through Plante's teammates, a swirl of color and flying ice roaring down toward the goal, thousands screaming as the stick cracks against a frozen rubber disk that gets smaller and harder as it hurtles at one hundred miles an hour toward Jacques Plante's throat.

Slap.

Time stands still, and thousands catch their breaths as Plante's big glove flicks out and kills the puck in its leather folds. Plante sinks to his knees, drawing out the last bit of emotional suspense. Then, as the breaths explode in a mighty *whoosh*, he disdainfully flips the puck away and watches the mad scramble start again.

"You must be born a goal tender, a man alone," said Plante one day over lunch. "Even the rule book says you are not a hockey player, that a team is made of five hockey players and a goal tender. You are a man who can prevent defeat, but you cannot win a game.

"The eyes are upon you; you are the target of the game. When a goal is scored, play stops and people talk. They say how you missed the puck, how you made a mistake. They do not talk of all the mistakes that were made before the opposing player took his shot. They say it is your mistake alone."

Across the table, Plante looked like a man born to accept such responsibility. He was thirty-four years old at the time, recently traded to New York, after nine seasons with Montreal. His face was strong and angular, with deep hollows beneath the scarred cheekbones and a quick mobility around the eyes and the mouth.

During a game, the face, which bears the marks of several hundred stitches, is covered with a 10-ounce, padded plastic mask. He introduced the mask to the National Hockey League in 1959 because, he admitted freely, he was tired of seeing his blood on the ice.

"During the game itself there is little time to be afraid. Once you are afraid in a game, you are through," he said in a clipped accent bearing traces of his native French.

"But I was not sleeping at night, replaying each game in my head—the pucks I stopped, and the ones that missed my head by an inch—thinking about more stitches and going back to the hospital. And wasn't four times enough for one nose to be broken?"

So he began wearing the mask in practice sessions. Then one night in New York, a Ranger backhanded a shot into the left side of Plante's nose. Jake the Snake went down.

The crowd waited impatiently for twenty minutes, while the game was held up so seven stitches could be taken on Plante's nose. When he skated out again, he was wearing his ghoulish Plexiglas mask.

A controversy began. Originally the Montreal coach said Plante might wear his mask only until his nose healed. But Plante refused to take it off. Fans called him a coward, but Plante was impervious to catcalls from the safe seats. Some hockey people felt the mask was unseemly and detrimental to a goalie's performance. Others thought it sensible and humane.

Montreal won its next eleven games. The mask stayed.

"I am the best goalie in the league," Plante said, "and with the mask I am even better. I can laugh at getting hit in the face. I can use my face to stop pucks."

A perennial winner of the best goalie award, Plante is widely imitated by youngsters throughout Canada. The mask soon became standard equipment, and Plante's innovative style of play was quickly copied. Unlike most goalies, who stay close to the net, Plante wanders—he moves around, plays the angles instead of the net, skates out to make saves and pass the puck, and shouts instructions at the defensemen.

For all his activity, agility, and grandstanding, Plante's biggest problem has always been breathing. He was raised in Shawinigan Falls, Quebec, and severe asthma kept him from competitive sports until he was in his teens. The son of a machinist, Jacques was the eldest of a large family, and he diapered, sewed, and cleaned for the brood.

Until he was fourteen years old, he slept sitting up, coughing all night, falling asleep at dawn when he was too tired to cough anymore. When he was fourteen, Jacques' condition improved, and he began playing hockey. He became winded too quickly to skate very long, so he played at goal.

The asthma has bothered him throughout his career, but he does not like to talk about it—although he admits that it must seem crazy for a man to leave his wife and children and such hobbies as oil painting and knitting to stand on ice and try to stop pucks.

"I worked very hard to get to the top, and now that I am here, I want to enjoy it, to taste it," he said.

"And there are those nights I go home, and I tell my wife I don't know how they could score; I filled the net tonight, I blocked it all, and every time they shot I scooped up the puck and laughed 'Aha, look what I found.' Nights like that keep me going, on nights like that I know I love what I do."

III

Dorold's Own Starlet II
Is a Fat Little Dog

A fat little pug named Dorold's Own Starlet II wiped her nose on Mrs. Elizabeth Keil's red jersey skirt.

"I think she's a little let down," said Mrs. Keil, dabbing at her own moist blue eyes. "Everybody's crazy about Starlet except the judges."

"Starlet's a nice little dog," I said to Mrs. Keil, and she brightened a little. We were sitting in a dim corner of the basement of Madison Square Garden. Upstairs, the annual Westminster Dog Show was in progress. Earlier in the day, Dorold's Own Starlet II had finished fourth in the open class for fawn bitches, but the rules forbade an owner from taking a dog home until the show was over, and so Mrs. Keil, a plump, pleasant, middle-aged woman, sat on a wooden chair in the basement and tried to keep smiling.

She was a widow, she said, and not a very good mixer, so she just watched the swirling crowd of people and animals. Slim, delicate young men snipped invisible hairs from the rumps of shaven poodles, and chilly, handsome booted blondes were towed through the aisles by lean, stalking whippets. A fat, small woman with a little green bow in her hair was tying an identical little green bow onto her Pekingese.

"I'm really not so disappointed," said Mrs. Keil, "because Starlet is only a pet—the only dog I have. It would be nice for her to win first place, but it's not so important."

Mrs. Keil said she lived alone in Kew Gardens, Queens, and had bought Starlet eighteen months earlier because she had heard that pugs were very affectionate and not particularly active. She had taken a bus to Englishtown, New Jersey, and had bought Starlet for two hundred dollars, from a recommended kennel. A lady friend had helped her lug the dog home on the bus.

A woman at the kennel rather pointedly told Mrs. Keil that she hoped all of Starlet's "good training wouldn't go to pot." The dog was ten months old at the time and had won a few ribbons at some small shows.

Mrs. Keil thought about that for a long time. She felt she did have a responsibility to Starlet's breeding and training, but it would be so difficult: She had no car, no children, not much extra money to spend on so expensive a hobby. When Mr. Keil was alive—he had died five years earlier—there was usually a dog around the house, but not for show.

Once, she remembered mistily, they had a little wirehaired terrier, who had walked in one day out of a summer storm. Mrs. Keil had called him Puppy because she didn't expect to keep him very long and she didn't want to impose a name on his next owner. Puppy stayed with the Keils for seven years—until he died of a heart attack two months before Mr. Keil died.

"I never would have thought to name her Dorold's Own Starlet II, but she had the name already," said Mrs. Keil.

Early last year, said Mrs. Keil, she had taken Starlet to some local shows, by bus and subway, carrying her in a suitcase that weighed sixteen and a half pounds when the dog was inside. She had won some ribbons. At the Westminster show, Mrs. Keil had paid a professional handler to lead Starlet into the ring because she becomes nervous when the judges give her instructions. She said each trip by a professional handler cost between twenty and thirty dollars.

Mrs. Keil seemed a little out of place at the Garden, surrounded by all the expensive-looking dogs with their expensive-looking people, a lady with an apron over her Pucci dress, the fresh-faced, outdoorsy girls in flat shoes, cardigan sweaters, and *Distemper Fighter* buttons.

I left Mrs. Keil for a few minutes and wandered over to a booth where a woman was selling twenty-five-dollar dog coats.

"We want her dog to look as smart as madame," the saleswoman was saying, holding up a pink cocktail coat of embroidered silk with a mohair lining.

I asked her, "When would a dog wear that?"

She raised her eyebrow and replied, "After five o'clock."

When I returned, Mrs. Keil was still on her wooden chair, peering down at Starlet, who was cuddling against her red skirt, froglike eyes alert, little curly piglike tail at rest. Mrs. Keil told me that Starlet has an electric-blue coat with a mink collar, but only wears it to keep warm.

A woman passed us and smiled down at Starlet. "Such a dood little dirl," she said. "She's so fat."

Mrs. Keil put on a pair of eyeglasses she had borrowed

from a neighbor in Queens—her own were broken, she said—and looked at little fat Starlet.

"Oh, my goodness," said Mrs. Keil. "Maybe that's what the judges thought too."

IV

Two Champions: Dick Tiger and Joey Giardello

A raw December wind whipped Atlantic City as I hurried along the ocean boardwalk toward my first championship prizefight. I felt very keen and alert, and a little nervous too. This was 1963. I had been on the *Times* for more than six years, but I was just starting out as the new boxing reporter, and I wanted to do well on this story. I would be covering boxing for almost four more years, until I began writing the "Sports of the Times" column. I would be covering many fights more important than this middleweight title bout between Dick Tiger and Joey Giardello, and I would cover them in more exciting places than this summer resort shuttered for the winter. But I would never be quite so keyed up again.

I had spent a great deal of time talking with each of the fighters, and I didn't know who I wanted to win. I had first met the champion, Dick Tiger, in New York, while he was in training for an earlier fight. He had looked almost comical then, moving down Eighth Avenue on the balls of his feet like a big black cat, a homburg perched on the top of his head. The homburg was too small for him, but it was years before I learned that he always bought his hats a size too small so he could share them with his brothers back home in Nigeria.

134

As we walked down Eighth Avenue, his manager was saying, "African fighters are very good, very tough. They're closer to the jungle."

"There is no jungle in Nigeria," said Tiger without smiling.

"It's just an expression, Dick, just a figure of speech," said the manager hastily. "I mean they're hungry fighters."

Tiger bounced on down Seventeenth Street and up three flights of stairs in the Catholic Youth Organization building. We followed him through a clean, brightly lit gym and into the dressing room.

As the homburg, the light-brown sports jacket, the white shirt, and the blue tie disappeared into a rusty metal locker, Tiger seemed to grow larger, to shed the comedy of his clothes. The blue tribal tattoos across his chest and back rippled over knotty muscle and made him seem suddenly savage.

But there was only gentleness in his eyes, and humor twitched at the corners of his mouth. I watched him tape his hands with great care, slowly, first winding the bandages around and around, then placing the sponge across the knuckles, then wrapping on the adhesive. Very few champions tape their own hands, and I asked him why he didn't have his manager or trainer take care of this daily chore.

"I am a traveling man, and I got to do things myself; a fighter should know these things," he said. "This is my business."

It had been his business for eleven years then, since

he had become a professional fighter at the age of twenty-three. He told me that he was born in Amaigbo, a remote eastern Nigerian town in the rain forests of the Binin River Delta. He was raised on a farm and educated at an Anglican mission school, where classes were held in his tribal language, Ibo, as well as in English. At nineteen he went to the city of Aba to work in his brother's grocery store. At a local boys' club he learned to box.

He had been christened Richard Ihetu—Ibo for "what I want"—but when he began fighting professionally he took the ring name Dick Tiger. His opponents included Easy Dynamite, Black Power, and Mighty Joe Young. He beat them all and attracted the attention of British boxing promoters. But lonely and cold in the dank gyms of London and Liverpool, he lost his first four fights in Britain.

Letters from his family in Nigeria were beseeching him to give up the foolishness and return to his father's farm or his brother's grocery store. Tiger gave himself one more chance. In his fifth fight, he knocked out a Liverpool boy in ninety seconds, and Richard Ihetu, farmer and clerk, was gone forever.

"That was it, man. Oh, that was it," he said nostalgically, years later, as he finished taping his hands for the afternoon's workout.

Dick Tiger worked harder in the gym than any other fighter I have ever seen. He believed that the foundation of his success was good physical condition. He could hit hard but so could many middleweights; his boxing skills improved each year, but he always lacked finesse. But

Dick Tiger had never been knocked down, and no fighter had ever tired him out in the ring. Dick Tiger would stand and fight all day if necessary and let his opponent wear himself out.

"Whenever I'm tired," Tiger once told me, "I know my opponent is tired too. He's used up his strength just trying to hit me."

"That Tiger, he works like a horse, a real workhorse he is," said Jimmy August, the fat little trainer, as we walked into the gym. "All business. He knows God built him like a horse, and he works like one. That right, Dick?"

"The gloves," said Tiger, holding out his taped hands. All business. There was no small talk for Tiger in the gym.

For two hours Tiger worked hard, ignoring the youngsters in the gym and the curious Catholic Youth Organization workers. Silver globules of sweat broke out on his forehead and ran together in streams down his body. Everything he did was methodical and intense, the rope slapping rhythmically under his feet, the light punching bag rattling twenty times at a clip against its wooden support, the heavy canvas-covered bag groaning and creaking at his left hooks, the floor of the gym complaining as the chunky 5-foot 8-inch fighter twisted his neck until his eyes popped and wrenched his torso and strained his legs and gave every blood vessel, bone, and muscle in his body a reason to jump out of its skin.

He had always worked hard. He was never a spectacular fighter or a controversial personality, so it took years for him to become established and get frequent fights.

He first came to the United States in 1959 and lived in third-rate Manhattan hotels with his pregnant wife, cooking meals on a hot plate and running in nearby Central Park while he slowly gained the reputation among boxing people of an honest workman. His wife gave birth to twins and then to a third child in 1960. Tiger sent her back to Nigeria and began commuting between New York and Aba. He saved his money very carefully, walked whenever possible, and window-shopped for entertainment.

Late in 1962 he won the middleweight title from Gene Fullmer, and except that now he had more money to bring home to Abigail, his wife, very little changed. And he was still working harder than anyone else.

At the end of his two-hour workout, Tiger showered and dressed, shrinking back into his clothes, topping himself with his homburg. I did not think he looked comical any longer. On our way out of the gym, a huge, red-faced policeman shook hands with Tiger and wished him luck.

"Are the constables in Nigeria as big as him?" asked Jimmy August, like a straight man feeding a line to a comedian.

"Sure," said Tiger, smiling, " 'cause for breakfast they eat guys like him."

Everyone laughed, and Jimmy August poked me in the ribs. "Whatta sense of humor. Couple years ago, this reporter whose name I won't mention asked Dick if he was a cannibal, and Dick said, 'Not anymore, I quit after eating the governor-general and getting a bellyache.'"

We laughed some more and headed toward the subway at Eighth Avenue. Tiger said he felt very good, that he always felt good after a hard workout.

"This is my business," he said. "I work very hard at it now because it will not always be my business. I want to make money. I want six hundred thousand dollars. Now, all I have is a house and a Peugeot car, but I will have more houses and factories and shops."

He said that people in America did not realize how modern Nigeria was, that there were tall buildings in the capital, Lagos. People thought Nigeria was all jungle, he said, and filled with tigers.

"The only tiger I ever saw," he said, "was in a cage in the Liverpool Zoo."

*   *   *

I met Joey Giardello a few days before the fight. I had gone to Atlantic City early, to spend time with the two fighters, and the first morning there I visited Giardello in his hotel room. He was lying, fully dressed, across his bed, running a square hand through his crisp, curly black hair. He was smiling, the lines of his face folding into the network of scar tissue around his eyes, and he was saying softly, "My daddy was champion of the world. My daddy was champion of the world."

He turned on his side and faced me. "In just a few days I start a new life; it's gonna make everything worthwhile. People are gonna look at me different; they're not gonna call me the bad boy of boxing no more. They're not gonna think I'm just an East Side kid who likes to bang heads.

"And my three sons, they're gonna be able to say 'My daddy was champion of the world.' "

Giardello said he knew that Tiger was a three to one favorite to win the fight, but that he was desperate.

"This is it for me, I busted my back to get this shot for the title. I'm thirty-three years old, and people can talk about Joey Giardello; they can say he did a lot, and he won a lot of fights, and he had everything in boxing except the big one, except the title. Saturday I get the title."

People had always talked a lot about Joey Giardello, and some of the things they said made him angry. People who knew him back in Brooklyn, where he was born Carmine Tilelli, remembered him as a tough kid nicknamed Chubby who was only afraid of one thing—that someone would think he was chicken. When he was fifteen years old, using the draft card of a friend's cousin, he joined the army, where he volunteered for the paratroopers and learned to box. Carmine Tilelli was never heard from again. The name on the draft card was Joseph Giardello, and Chubby kept it even after his discharge.

After the army, he began fighting professionally out of South Philadelphia, his new home, never getting into really serious trouble, but scraping along with a tough crowd. He was a great natural fighter, he hit hard, he could take punishment, and he was fast, clever, and tricky. If he would ever settle down and get himself into good shape, the boxing experts said, Joey could be champion. But he liked to drink beer and eat ravioli and stay up late and gamble, and he hated to run in the morning and sweat in the afternoon. There were many rumors about Joey's being involved with gangsters and fixed fights, but nothing was ever proven although he was barred from fighting in some states for a while. In 1954 he was sent to jail for beating up a gas-station attendant. He always maintained that he was framed.

He turned again on the bed and stared at the ceiling. "My past, my past, always they talk about my past. I got an eleven-year-old boy who doesn't know his daddy was in jail. I got a ten-year-old who's mentally retarded. Someday I got to explain a lot of things to them about their father, about the dumb things he did. When I tell them those things I want to be able to tell them that their daddy won the title. I want to give them something, maybe something to say when other kids call them names or make fun of their father. I want them to be able to say 'My daddy was champion of the world.' "

*   *   *

The day of the fight dawned gloriously clear and bright. A warm winter sun rose over the ocean. At noon the traditional weigh-in ceremony was held in Convention Hall, where the fight would be held that night. Both fighters were grim and edgy. Giardello weighed 158 pounds, two less than he had to for a middleweight fight, and everybody was pleasantly surprised at how lean and firm he looked. Could it be true, they asked, that Joey had really given up beer, ravioli, and cigarettes for this fight? I remember thinking that Dick Tiger must have believed it was true. Always the politest of men, he seemed surly at the weigh-in, and he snapped at the photographers, "No more pictures, no more foolishness."

Then both fighters left to eat their steak dinners and rest until fight time. I talked to a few people who had just arrived from New York. The word was out that Joey would fall apart around the fifth round, his legs and his stomach would never hold out against the tough old Tiger. After all, hadn't Tiger's manager allowed him to take this fight because Joey was washed up?

I went back to my hotel to write my early story.

When I came out again, it was dark, and a chill had settled on the city. The wind on the boardwalk carried salt and sand. I went into the arena early and watched it fill up with men in blue suits and gray coats and pearl hats—and scars. By the time the fight began, every light bulb in the place had its own halo of cigar smoke.

It was a beautiful fight. Joey Giardello rose from the ashes of his past like the mythical phoenix, forcing the action from the start with flurries of left jabs, dancing around the baleful Tiger who stalked him relentlessly. But it was like stalking the wind.

Nothing worked for Tiger that night. He always tried to force his opponents into corners where he could work on their stomachs, but Joey slipped away from the punches and whirled out of tight spots.

After five rounds the crowd settled back to wait for Joey's legs to buckle, for his chest to start heaving, for the superbly conditioned Tiger to drive him into the canvas. But Giardello seemed to get stronger, bouncier as the fight went on, taking the belly punches and giving solid head shots in return. As the fight moved into the later rounds, an electric hum filled the arena. Joey was winning; he was on the verge of scoring the most incredible upset of the year.

His friends from Brooklyn were screaming "Take 'im, Chubby, take 'im" and his friends from South Philadelphia were screaming "Jo-Jo, baby, Jo-Jo, baby" all through the eleventh, twelfth, thirteenth, and fourteenth rounds as both fighters forgot strategy and style and stood toe to toe and belted and pummeled each other. Joey was bleeding and Tiger's face was a twisted mask as they stepped out for the last round, the fifteenth. Only a knockout would win for Tiger.

"Stay away from him, Joey; you're the champion," screamed a man in Giardello's corner, and Joey began to weep in the ring as he danced away from the stalking Tiger for the last three minutes before the referee raised his right arm, and Joey's sons could say "My daddy is champion of the world."

*   *   *

The next morning Dick Tiger was polite but critical. He said that Giardello did more dancing than boxing, more running away than fighting. And Joey, laughing and joyous, said that he would give Tiger a chance to win the title back very soon and that he had learned a great lesson. He would stay in the top physical condition that had given him the endurance to become champion, he said. Roadwork every morning, early bedtime every night. No beer. No cigarettes. No pasta. Joey Giardello would never be fat and breathless again.

It was my first championship prizefight, so I can be forgiven for believing him.

*   *   *

Joey enjoyed being champion; he was generous to charities, kind to his family, and patient with strangers. But I think he enjoyed it most in the Passyunk Street Gym in South Philadelphia, where he trained. It was a dank and dirty place, on a crowded winding street of taverns and small shops. He would spring up the splintery wooden steps that led to the second-floor pool hall, throw open the door, tap the bouncer on the belly, and call "Hey, Weasel, what's the number, Weasel?"

The skinny kids around the pinball machines would turn, their cuesticks frozen over the pool tables, and a chorus would answer, "Josie, how are ya, Josie?"

Giardello would wave and spin out the door again with a cheery "Gotta go train, see ya later," knowing that they would all stop what they were doing and follow him upstairs to the third-floor gym, the middleweight king's throne room. He would change into gym clothes, drape a white terry-cloth robe over his shoulders, and reappear, his eyes glittering alertly out of a lump-putty face.

"Good to see ya, how ya been," he says to the crowd, climbing through the ropes, starting to shadowbox. The phone rings in a corner of the small room. "It's for Salvatore," a kid calls. Joey stops shadowboxing.

"Salvatore, Salvatore, the phone, go answer it." And then he spins and snuffles, punching at his invisible enemy. The gym door creaks open, and a latecomer tries to sneak in. "Well, good morning, Ziggy," says Joey, "didya just get up?"

He finishes shadowboxing and leans over the ring ropes.

"Hey," he calls to a stocky middle-aged man, "how come ya never let me over the bridge for free?"

"I can't, Joey, it comes outa my pocket if I do."

"Ahhhh!" Joey grins, a mouthful of bad teeth.

"I swear it, Joey, I shouldn't see tomorrow."

"Ya knockin' down much?"

"Are you crazy, Joey? It ain't worth it. I got a lifetime job, six thousand dollars a year."

Joey nods, understanding, and begins belting a heavy bag so ratty that an army duffel bag has been fitted over it to keep in the stuffing. After a while, bored, he merely stops working out, showers, gets dressed again, and wanders back down to the pool hall for a paper cup of tea and a Lucky Strike from one of his wife's cousins.

"It ain't the fanciest place in the world," Joey says to me, "but it's nice to have your friends around."

*   *   *

The second championship fight between Giardello and Tiger was held in New York, and we were all two years older. Especially Joey. He was fighting from memory.

Giardello never had it that night, weak-kneed in the early rounds against Tiger's rush, game in the middle rounds as he took brief advantage of Tiger's lapses, sometimes even fierce in the later rounds, but far too tired to

follow up his punches. Joey's courage was never in question—only his reflexes.

"Use style, Joe, he's too strong for you," Giardello's
trainer screamed over the beat of an *etulago*, a Nigerian
drum that thundered for Tiger from the end balcony.

But Joey, a battered, hard-used thirty-five, could barely
get up the style, catching left hooks he would have
ducked two years before, pushing out his own left jab as
if he were going for the boardinghouse potatoes. Later
on in his dressing room Giardello would tell us that he
had trained too hard for the fight in an effort to please his
first New York audience in nine years. This was far from
my first championship prizefight, and I didn't believe him
at all. Besides, from the start of the fight I saw how his
pale soft belly leaked over his black trunks.

Tiger had gone for that belly from the opening bell,
to the cheers of a crowd of more than seventeen thousand.
This was a Tiger crowd. They cheered the Nigerian right
through the early rounds as he cut open the left side of
Joey's head and slammed him wobbly. Joey's jaw hung
slack, and he was walking flat-footed.

The *etulago* picked up the beat as Tiger drove Joey up
against the ropes and speared him with short uppercuts
that left spreading red welts on his chest. The crowd
roared with a bloodlust that never fails to frighten me at
prizefights, and the reporters at ringside all nodded—
Joey was finished; he'd be lucky to get through the fifth
round.

Joey was finished. We knew it. The crowd knew it.
Tiger knew it. But Joey came back in the fifth, winning

the round with three ripping punches that rocked Tiger's head, and he belted Tiger in the sixth, and he started building up momentum in the seventh. The crowd was roaring, but it was roaring for Joey now, Joey the cutie pie who wasn't going to lose his championship easily, Joey the bad boy who had waited a long time to show the world that he could take it on the chin and keep coming back for more. I remember looking up at the two fighters from my ringside seat and thinking that Joey was truly a tough man; he had come back from a jail sentence, from the tragedy of a retarded son, from his own weaknesses.

Late in the seventh round, Tiger shoved Joey up against the ropes, banged his head from side to side, let him spin into a short chopping right, and then slammed him back into the ropes. He raked Joey across the ropes until a rope burn on his back sprang blood.

People in the crowd closed their eyes, and some of them prayed that Joey would get knocked out right then, before he got hurt.

But Joey was not going to be knocked out. Pride kept him upright. He was going to lose his championship, but he was going to lose it standing up. At the start of the fifteenth and final round, he leaned toward Tiger and said, "Nice fight." When it was over, the crowd stood and cheered them both.

*   *   *

Tiger didn't hold the title too long after that. He was more than thirty-six years old now, and he was having trouble with his weight. A middleweight must fight at one hundred and sixty pounds or less, and as a boxer grows older, he finds it more and more difficult to keep his weight down without sacrificing his strength. In the spring of 1966, Tiger lost his title to Emile Griffith—a younger man and a welterweight who had been having trouble staying at one hundred and forty-seven pounds. With consummate logic, Tiger decided to move up in class too. In the winter of 1966, he beat José Torres and became light-heavyweight champion. I talked to him the morning after that fight, and he was still the traveling philosopher in a cheap hotel room. "The people all said that Tiger is finished, that he looks one hundred years old," Dick said, "and now they come around to pat my head and tell me I'm a good boy. That's life."

Giardello, meanwhile, was getting fatter and fatter, drifting in and out of semiretirement for fights with ham-and-eggers, which he sometimes lost. But he always got a big hand in the Garden when he climbed through the ropes to be introduced before the main event as a former champion. He had had it, and no one could ever take it away.

*   *   *

In March of 1968, Tiger arrived in New York to start training for his fight with Bob Foster. He was very upset. He sat in an overheated room in a cheap Manhattan hotel, his square hands opening and closing and plucking at his baggy gray pants, his voice rising, his mouth twisted. "I used to be a happy man," he said, "but now I have seen something I have never seen before. I read about killings and war, but I had never seen such things. Now I have seen massacres."

He bounded from the straight-backed chair and began fishing in his bureau drawers, through pamphlets and books and newspaper clippings. "Ah, here," he said, almost reverently opening some tissue paper. "This is Aba." He spread the photographs on the bed.

"The hospital. There were eight patients and a doctor when the planes came and threw bombs around. Hired pilots. The Nigerians can't fly planes. They are a thousand years behind civilization, that is why they are doing everything wrong.

"The open market, look at that. In that corner, that is a hand. A little girl's hand. What does she know of war? This woman burned. These men dead, not even soldiers. That is a woman too. No, it is not rags; it was a woman."

He carefully repacked the photographs and sat down again. "The Nigerian radio says Dick Tiger of Nigeria will defend his light-heavyweight championship. Dick Tiger of Nigeria. They still claim me, and they would kill me; they want to kill us all. I am a Biafran. I am Dick Tiger of Biafra. And we just want to live."

Tiger's view of the Nigeria-Biafra war was as straightforward as the pamphlets in his room. In 1966 thousands of Ibo tribesmen were slaughtered in pogroms in northern Nigeria. The Christian Ibos were civil servants and small businessmen in the Muslim north. The Ibos fled back to their eastern native lands and ultimately formed a new country, Biafra.

Under the slogan *To Keep Nigeria One*, federal troops

attacked Biafra, murdering, looting, wasting, and starving their countrymen.

"Keep Nigeria one," spat Tiger derisively. "What will be left for them to rule if they keep killing our children?"

Tiger said he had moved his family, which now included seven children, from Aba, where he owned houses, cinemas, factories, and shops, to Amaigbo, the remote delta town of his birth. At thirty-eight, he had volunteered for the Biafran army, teaching physical fitness and acting as an inspiration. He gave no exhibitions because groups of soldiers dared not congregate for fear of strafing attacks.

"I do not worry so much anymore," said Tiger, restless on his wooden chair. "The children have learned to take cover quickly when they hear the bomber planes. It is the fighter planes we worry about. The bombs fall slowly. If you see them, you can run away. But you never see the bullets."

*   *   *

The fight with Bob Foster ended in the fourth round. It looked like a mismatch. Foster was 6 feet 3½ inches tall, nearly eight inches taller than Tiger, and at 173¼ he was more than five pounds heavier. Foster was twenty-nine; Tiger thirty-nine. Even at that, it would have been a fair fight two years earlier—even a year earlier. But not even the magnificent fighting machine that Tiger had built and maintained so carefully over the years could last forever. I saw Tiger fight again after that night, and I saw him win, but I knew then that Tiger was very near the end of the road.

In the fourth round, Foster threw a long right that Tiger pulled away from, and in doing so, his head collided with a left hook. Tiger went straight down, his head smacked the canvas with a sickening thump, and he twitched on his back like a turtle on its shell. He had to be helped up.

As he left the ring the announcer said, "Let's give Dick Tiger a nice hand, folks." Simply and a little sheepishly, Tiger raised his arms and shrugged.

One of the first visitors to his dressing room was Joey Giardello.

"Hey, Dick, you all right?"

"Ah, Jo-ee," said Tiger, beaming. "Yes. I am fine."

"What you gonna do now, Dick?"

"Eat a big dinner. I am very hungry, and, thank God, I can eat."

Joey smiled, the concern in his face disappearing among the scuffs and lumps and marks, and he shook his head in wonderment.

The dressing room was jammed. In one corner a fight manager named Yancey Durham was telling a group that "Tiger was caught by an ordinary hook, merely ordinary."

In another corner an African student with a British accent explained to his group, "Now that I have analyzed it, he was struck down by a jab." The student threw a slow right uppercut toward his admirers, who nodded and murmured. Reporters whispered among themselves about the terrible pressure Tiger was under to make money to help the Biafran cause—everything he had worked for had been blown up by the Nigerians, and his family was hiding in the rain forests. A youngster with slicked-down yellow hair was pushed into Tiger's arms by his father, and the flashbulb on a Kodak Instamatic camera exploded.

"Gentlemen," said Tiger, smiling, "I am sorry. But for all these years I have been knocking people out, and now I know what it's like getting knocked out. And now that he has knocked me out, I think Foster is the best fighter in the whole world."

Tiger took the youngster's hand. "You're a nice boy. Shake hands with a loser."

In a corner, Joey Giardello whispered, "I can't hear him—did he say he was gonna retire? No, huh. Some guy, that Tiger, what a guy."

Tiger apologized again for losing, and said, "That's business." We asked him if thoughts of his country and of his family had weighed him down. He said No. He insisted that he had been able to push all such thoughts aside while he prepared for the fight, and only now that it was all over would he allow himself to think about his family and country.

And then he looked around his crowded dressing room, a smile growing as he saw the sleek Joey and Yancey and the chattering Africans and the reporters and the slicked-down youngster and his father; and Tiger said, "You know, since I been winning I never had my fans stay in my dressing room so long. Now, I'm a loser, and everybody's here. I guess I am a good man."

V

Winter Thoughts of a Bush-League Ballplayer

Jerry Rosenthal is over thirty now, and the call will never come. Once, not so long ago, whenever the first soft fingers of spring stretched over the points of the city, Jerry Rosenthal would move nearer his telephone and frame his answer to the man who would say "We need a second baseman, kid. You available?"

He would wait, and he would think about his two and a half summers in the bush leagues, the boredom, the weariness, the long hours in a cramped station wagon, the poor pay, and the sparse crowds. He would remember a day in Lewiston, Idaho, when a ground ball skipped between his legs into the outfield, driving home the winning run. He had looked for a fat blade of grass to hide under.

But he would also remember a day in Yakima, Washington, sitting on the bench with a slow-healing broken cheekbone, when the manager sent him up to bat because everyone else was hurt or out of the game. He belted the second pitch into the left-field stands for a homerun.

"We need a second baseman, kid. You available?"

Sure, I'm available, he would have to say. I've been available since I was ten years old and imagined my face on a bubble-gum card, since summers in high school when I played on three different semipro teams at once, since the winter of 1960, when I signed a contract with the Milwaukee Braves on the dining-room table of my parents' home in Brooklyn.

Jerry Rosenthal was twenty-one at the time, and the future was a straight path to the Hall of Fame. He had one month to go at Hofstra University, where he had maintained a *B* average in class and a .408 average at bat. The contract carried a bonus of twenty-two thousand dollars, and when he signed it, his mother and sisters kissed him tearfully; his father, brother, and the scout shook his hand; and someone gave him a glass of Scotch. It tasted awful, he remembered.

And that was the start of his education.

"I was a gee-whiz kid," he told me one afternoon, years later. "All my life I'd thought about the glamour of professional baseball. I got to spring training in Georgia, and the food was lousy, and after you'd seen the movie, there was nothing else to do that week. But I learned the language."

He learned that year to call a baseball by its rightful name (*seed, pea, potato*) and that the worst accusation you can make of a ballplayer is that he chokes (*fails in the clutch*). A fine thing to say to an umpire was "Shake yourself, meat, your eyes are stuck."

He was assigned to Eau Claire, Wisconsin, of the Northern League, a team that traveled in three station wagons. They would finish a night game in Duluth, Minnesota, at 11:30 P.M., be on the road by midnight, and reach Aberdeen, South Dakota, by 2 P.M. the following day. A poor sleeper in station wagons, he became an authority on the Northern Lights.

"The next year I went to Yakima," he said, "and by this time I couldn't understand why people thought I led an exciting life.

"Baseball is three hours of tense excitement, but the rest of it is hanging around or traveling. I hate to play cards, and managers don't like players to go to the beach. You can see only so many afternoon cartoon festivals before you go out of your mind. I used to spend a lot of time reading in the public library. A lot of players thought I was crazy."

He became a little cynical, he said, about spitballs and emery balls and sign-stealing by telescope. He found out that bench jockeys weren't really vicious at all; they just made noise to keep themselves awake. He got into a lot of fights in Yakima because he had a manager who demanded that everyone run out on the field, swinging, after a bean ball. Anyone who stayed out of the brawl was fined fifty dollars. And he found out that fighting was kind of fun—it loosened everyone up.

He learned that the bullpen is the best place to pick up girls and that keeping one's mouth shut is a good general policy. There were a lot of pressures in the bush leagues and a lot of strange men living under them. He met some of the heroes of his Ebbets Field boyhood and was shocked by their skinny legs and potbellies and empty minds.

"Major league baseball players are not gods," he said.

"They're just men in kids' uniforms."

He ran a strong, square hand through his reddish-blond hair. "Baseball is a business, not a national pastime. People came out to the ball park on nights we had cow-milking contests and fireworks. When we were battling for first place, you could count the crowd between innings."

In the middle of the season at Yakima, Jerry was batting over .300 and fielding well. During pre-game practice one day, a thrown ball bounced into the dugout and smashed his cheek and jaw. After an operation, he was out of action for eight weeks. He never regained his form. When the Braves reassigned him to Yakima the following year, he refused to report. He felt he was ready for a team in a higher minor league. The Braves did not. Reluctantly they gave him his release. A free agent, Jerry went home to Brooklyn to wait.

We talked one afternoon that summer, while he was still waiting, and I asked him if it was all worth it—all the boredom and the weariness and the long hours—if the call never came and he never got his chance to play in the major leagues.

"It was worth every minute of it," he said. "An athlete learns a little more about life than an intellectual. You learn to hang in there, to keep going when you're so fouled up you think you'll die.

"Every day is another challenge; you've got to prove yourself all over again. You're at second base and a two-hundred-twenty-pound catcher comes barreling in to bust up the double play. You can't run away; you just jump and throw that ball right into his face, and if he doesn't get out of the way, at least he'll never come in on you like that again."

He smiled. "A pitcher's struck you out five times, and you go up there knowing you can belt him. You made a bad error last inning, and now it's the crucial play of the game, and under your breath you ask the batter to hit the ball to you. That's hanging in there."

Jerry waited through the summer and through the following year, but the call did not come, and with each passing year the chance that it would ever come grew dimmer and dimmer until all hope was gone. Much later, we met at a boxing match. He had a good job and most of his bonus money, and he said he was very happy. A college graduate, a reader of books, he had spent summers in the bush leagues and learned to hang in there. He was way ahead of the game—except in the dying days of a cold hard winter, when the sky is streaked with springtime and the air is faintly touched with the smell of the outfield grass.

Format by Kohar Alexanian
Set in 11 pt Linotype Primer
Composed, printed and bound
by American Book–Stratford Press, Inc.
HARPER & ROW, PUBLISHERS, INC.